Theology
for Ministry

Theology
for Ministry

March 2004

Margaret Lavin,

Margaret Lavin

Dear Joe:

Thank you for your support and
encouragement in my ministry, and
many Blessings on your ministry to
Regis and the Jesuit Community,

With gratitude,
Meg

NOVALIS

Cover design and layout: Caroline Gagnon
Cover image: Digital Vision/Getty Images

Business Office:
Novalis
49 Front Street East, 2nd Floor
Toronto, Ontario, Canada
M5E 1B3

Phone: 1-877-702-7773 or (416) 363-3303
Fax: 1-877-702-7775 or (416) 363-9409
E-mail: cservice@novalis.ca
www.novalis.ca

National Library of Canada Cataloguing in Publication Data

Lavin, Margaret
    Theology for ministry / Margaret Lavin.

Includes bibliographical references.
ISBN 2-89507-407-0

    1. Pastoral theology–Catholic Church. I. Title.

BX1912.L39 2004   253   C2004-900694-0

The Scripture quotations contained herein are from the New Revised Standard Version of the Bible, copyrighted 1989 by the Division of Christian Education of the National Council of the Churches of Christ in the United States of America, and are used by permission. All rights reserved.

Printed in Canada.

We acknowledge the financial support of the Government of Canada through the Book Publishing Industry Development Program (BPIDP) for our publishing activities.

5   4   3   2   1   08   07   06   05   04

To Peter, Ken and Cathy

Contents

Preface

This book is intended for everyone involved in ministry. It deals with two subjects: the theology that grounds ministry, and the theological anthropology that grounds the minister. The latter does, of course, flow from the former, and an intentional emphasis on theological anthropology encourages us to appreciate the existential reality of the human person in relationship to God. Thus, while it is written from a Roman Catholic perspective, this work's theological and anthropological insights and conclusions will be of value to those who minister in other Christian contexts. It will also be valuable material for theological reflection in preparing candidates for ministry.

The book has evolved from my twenty years of ministerial experience, including high school chaplaincy, retreat work, and spiritual direction, and especially from teaching theology and helping to prepare candidates for all forms of church-mandated ministries. Recent events, however, stimulated its writing.

While facilitating an "Introduction to Ministry" course and preparing students for their final comprehensive exam in systematic theology for the Master of Divinity degree, I noticed that many students did not always grasp the deep structural relationship between theology and the practice of ministry. They tended to put theology into an academic box, and often missed seeing the value of systematic theology for ministerial praxis. Yet what they learned in theology was supposed to ground their ministry. It is essential that these two elements of theory and practice be integrated.

Recent trends in the Canadian Roman Catholic church also inspired me to write this book. In January 2001, Archbishop Marcel Gervais of Ottawa mandated lay people in his archdiocese to administer the sacraments of baptism and marriage, and to preside at funerals.[1] This is not a new phenomenon in the church, but such practices have usually been confined to remote areas. Now these practices are being mandated in urban faith communities because there are not enough ordained priests to serve them.

In September 1999, a directive from the Ontario Conference of Catholic Bishops outlined the necessary steps that should be taken to prepare lay people who want to serve in parishes. These directives, in a document titled *Lay Pastoral Associates in Parish Settings: Perspectives, Considerations and Suggestions,*[2] consider the urgent need to develop a new understanding of the possibilities of lay ministry in the church, and describe how formation for this ministry can take place. Of the three major components outlined in the document—theological formation, pastoral intervention, and spiritual integration—theological formation is the first requirement: "The lay pastoral associate needs to know the fundamental elements of the Christian faith and of the Catholic tradition, be able to express and explain it and desire to always deepen it."[3] This book addresses this need.

In its *Guidelines for the Employment of Lay Pastoral Ministers,*[4] the archdiocese of Toronto reminds us that all who are baptized in Christ are called to participate in the reign of God. These guidelines draw heavily upon the documents of Vatican II, specifically, The Dogmatic Constitution on the Church (*Lumen Gentium*),[5] which calls upon all who are baptized in Christ to co-operate in the "common undertaking with one heart." (*LG* IV, 30) The guidelines state:

> Our appreciation of Baptism as a call to ministry is not new. As Christians, we have been encouraged consistently by the Church to involve ourselves in spiritual and corporal works of mercy. What the Second Vatican Council has highlighted for us, however, is an understanding that this invitation to serve one another is the very essence of our identity as Christians. In the 'diversity of graces, ministries and works' we bring unity to the Body of Christ, because 'all these things are the work of one and the same Spirit.' (*LG* IV, 32)[6]

According to these documents, then, there is a special need among lay people to heed the call to ministry. However, the Catholic church does not have a history of calling lay people to ministry. There is a long history of lay volunteer support, and many documents address lay participation in the world as witnesses to their beliefs, but a call to ecclesial ministry is more specific. Lay people in the church today are asked to be more than volunteers. "These men and women have passed from a volunteer status in the construction of the Christian community to the status of professionals."[7]

A new reality is emerging in our experience of ministry. Men and women who are not ordained ministers are serving the church in a mandated way that is quite different from the apostolate of the laity. This group finds itself actively involved in ministry somewhere between the apostolate of the laity and ordained ministry. A new generation of ministers who are not laity, as far as the term is used and accepted in church circles, or religious or clergy are coming forward and being trained to serve the church and other religiously affiliated institutions.

Where is the support for these people in this shift in our tradition? I believe that many recent mandates and church proposals are being put forward in a theological and ecclesial vacuum. This new breed of "lay" Catholics (and the clergy and religious who work alongside them) is being asked to participate in something that has not been named as such in church tradition. The need for these men and women to serve the church arises in an ecclesial structure that is not yet able or willing to accept them in the fullness of baptismal ministry.

And so the pivotal reason for this book: I work with such men and women, I teach them, I worship with them, and I listen to their stories, their struggles, and their dreams. They are eager, passionate, and committed to serving their church, yet they often find themselves in unknown, and sometimes hostile, terrain. This is not surprising, and is often the consequence of forging a new reality. How can we help this new generation of ministers to find and establish their ministerial identity? How can we provide a foundation for this new reality? We do not need to look very far. Indeed, we need look no further than the untapped resources of our Christian faith, articulated in our theological and church tradition.

What, in our Christian theological tradition, can help us to name our new reality and to broaden our understanding of ministry in order to meet the current needs of the church? In many respects, the answer is staring us in the face. In our tradition, we see the human person as created in the image and likeness of God. We are related to the humanity of God in Jesus Christ. In theological terms, this view of the human person is "theological anthropology." A renewed and intentional interest in theological anthropology can provide us with the foundation for our new ministerial reality.

In highlighting this anthropological foundation, *Theology for Ministry* speaks not just to this specific group of people, but to everyone who is committed to the value of shared baptismal ministry in the unity of service, which is the essence of the church: clergy, religious, lay people, and those who, for the present time, find themselves somewhere in between, facing a new reality.

Introduction

Theology is the articulation of our understanding of God and of how God relates to us in our everyday reality. Whenever we express our faith, we are making a theological statement. Systematic theology attempts to understand the realities of faith articulated in the doctrinal tradition of the church community. Theology is not just about ideas, it is about how people, in their day-to-day relationships, express their belief in God. In doing theology, we strive to maintain a balance between how we *understand* traditional doctrines *about* God, and how we *experience* God in *relationship*.

Ministry contributes to this expression in a unique way. It is the nexus between what theology says about faith and how faith is practised in contemporary experience. The fields of theology and ministry challenge and contribute to each other. If theology speaks to its cultural context, then it is able to address current pastoral needs and can challenge our understanding of ministry. Similarly, the challenges of pastoral needs can call for a renewal in theology and a broadened understanding of the affirmations of our faith.

The new challenges that we are facing in ministry today affect our understanding of what it means to be church, and the forms of ministry that can best serve the People of God. Ministry is connected with service in the church; we cannot discuss one without the other.[1] Current pastoral needs require a broadened understanding of ministry in the church, and thereby create the need for a closer look at how theology contributes to ministry.

This book operates on three levels. On one level it outlines the major theological themes that ground our understanding of who we believe our God is, and who we believe we are in relationship to God. On another level, it draws out the pastoral implications of these theological themes. At a third level—perhaps its deepest level—it reminds us of who we are, and the ways in which each of us is called to minister. Our mandate to minister is embedded in our Christian understanding of the human condition. What is offered here is not simply an introduction to theology, however; nor is it simply a theology *of* ministry. It is, rather, a theological grounding *for* ministry. Each of the six chapters takes a major area of systematic theology and shows how understanding it grounds and affects our ministerial praxis.

The purpose of this book is to highlight the major anthropological themes of our Christian tradition evident in the doctrines of revelation, christology, and trinity, and to outline the implications of these doctrinal themes, especially as they relate to the sacramentality of our lives, and to how we minister as a church community. The goal of the book is to reflect on these themes theologically, and to present a perspective for ministerial practice that witnesses to the value of the human person as created in the image of God.

The inherent value of being created in the image of God is developed from the belief that our God is a God of love, and that this love is expressed in the relationship between God and the human person. This relational aspect of God is articulated in the doctrine of revelation, that is, in the self-disclosed Word of God in Jesus Christ, through the Holy Spirit. Our God is a personal God who has spoken to us in our humanity in the person of Jesus of Nazareth.

In the context of the Christian tradition, human experience is the challenge to develop a personal relationship with Jesus Christ. This is possible for us because of God's great act of love in the Incarnation. In the Incarnation, the Word of God assumes a human nature. In theological terms, this is referred to as the "hypostatic union." The result of this union is that the human person can participate in the infinite mystery of God. The significance of the hypostatic union unfolds in the theological articulation of who Jesus is for us as outlined in our christology.

The relational context of this divine/human encounter is further developed in the doctrine of the trinity, and in our understanding of the work of the Holy Spirit in the world. One of the central trinitarian themes used in this book, borrowed from eastern orthodoxy, is *perichoresis*. There is a mutual and reciprocal communion of being that constitutes the nature of God. As the trinity is three persons in eternal communion, we, too, are called to live in communion with one another.

In summary, the theological themes that the book uses to ground its theological anthropology are as follows: 1) the human person is created in the image of God; 2) this image is built upon the self-disclosure of a loving and personal God; 3) the core of this creation is in the union of the divine and the human in the hypostatic union; and 4) the fullness of the relationships that our creation calls us to is the perichoretic communion of the trinitarian nature of God.

The work also acknowledges that while the mysteries of revelation, the Incarnation, and the trinity are the central mysteries of our Christian faith, they can, at times, seem totally incomprehensible. It is often difficult to realize that such incomprehensible teachings can disclose much that is directly relevant to our everyday Christian living, and especially the activity of our ministry. In the hypostatic union, however, it has been revealed to us that the positive element of mystery is that the grace of our loving God helps us to understand these truths, and that we can participate in the infinite mystery of who God is for us because we are created in the image of God.

This study is, then, an intentional focus on theological anthropology to strengthen those who are involved in ministry, and to challenge the faith community to widen its mandate for those who can minister in its name. If ministry can serve as a nexus between theology and contemporary experience, then a renewed interest in theological anthropology can help in meeting some of the ministerial challenges presented by current pastoral needs.

If we are going to meet current church needs, then a broadened understanding of ministry is necessary. We cannot escape what is evolving in the area of ministry in the church today. Apart from the already established ministries, and some of the latest appeals for an expansion of lay ministry, we can also anticipate new ministries in the future, particularly in the areas of theology, teaching, preaching, physical and psychological healing, social relations, peacemaking, family life, and counselling. If we ignore the challenges of this expansion, then we are ignoring the ongoing renewal of the church itself.

Chapter 1

Theological Anthropology:
We Are Heirs of God

For all who are led by the Spirit of God are children of God. For you did not receive a spirit of slavery to fall back into fear, but you have received a spirit of adoption. When we cry, 'Abba! Father!' it is that very Spirit bearing witness with our spirit that we are children of God, and if children, then heirs, heirs of God and joint heirs with Christ—if, in fact, we suffer with him so that we may also be glorified with him.

(Rom 8:14-17)

Introduction

The teachings of the Second Vatican Council and of contemporary theology provide insights into our understanding of the human person that lay a foundation for the church's ministerial and social mission. These insights emphasize the human person as the starting point for reflection on our theological tradition. Recent discernment from such theological reflection calls for structural changes within the church by way of a renewed commitment and respect for the unique experience of all persons, especially those whose dignity and freedom have been discounted or devalued. These emphases and calls for change are consistent with doctrinal teaching, and they respect the primary commitment to all baptized Christians.

Ministry, as the service of each member of the church community to one another, and to the world, is an active principle of Christian anthropology. How we understand the human person determines how we minister, to whom we minister, and who is mandated to minister within the church community. What a community of faith believes about God's people is the basis for ministry and for how ministry is structured. Who ministers, and how Christian ministry is carried out, is Christian anthropology in action.

According to the Christian tradition, the most essential fact of humanity is that all people are created in the image of God and, because of this, each of us is endowed with the dignity and freedom that flows from God's grace and love, and salvation in Jesus Christ. In the past fifty years there has been a renewed emphasis on the dignity and freedom of the human person in relation to institutional structures, which has always been part of our scriptural, theological, and church tradition. Concern for the dignity and freedom of the human person as created in the image of God is the principal anthropological perspective of the Vatican II documents. The Pastoral Constitution on the Church in the Modern World (*Gaudium et Spes*) stipulates: "For its part, authentic freedom is an exceptional sign of the divine image within [the human person]."[1] Further, the Declaration on Religious Freedom (*Dignitatis Humanae*) states:

> A sense of the dignity of the human person has been impressing itself more and more deeply on the consciousness of contemporary [humanity]. And the demand is increasingly made that [people] should act on their own judgment, enjoying and making use of a responsible freedom, not driven by coercion, but motivated by a sense of duty.[2]

This emphasis is, in part, responsible for the focus of human experience as the starting point for theological reflection. This is not surprising, since it is only within the context of our lives that we can encounter the sacred reality of God. God is present to us, and any response on our part to this grace is a result of God's grace at work within us. We are created with an inherent capability to know and to love God. This is part of who God has created us to be. In theological terms, this is called our capacity for self-transcendence, which is our ability to know, within the limits of our humanity, the God who created us and who is present to us.

Personhood, and the dignity and freedom of each person, is not the same as individualism, however. One who seeks to be an authentic person, reflecting God's image, is one who lives with others in community and who seeks to serve others, not themselves. Such a person can never be an isolated individual. Unfortunately, self-worth and the struggle for personal freedom are at times perceived by others as egocentric individualism. Often an institution, whether it be family, church, or state, accuses people of seeking what it perceives as an individualism when particular members are actually struggling toward the dignity and freedom that is their birthright because they have been created in the image of God.

Such accusations are usually made in proportion to the amount of control or power that the institution wants to maintain over its members. Both the person who seeks an individualism instead of mutual relationship, and the institution that refuses to honour mutual relations, fall into the trap of a self-serving ideology that is contrary to the message of the Christian tradition. When people genuinely seek to live the fullness of their personhood—which can, indeed, sometimes bring them into conflict with institutions—they are not on an egotistical quest. Likewise, when institutions sincerely reach out to their members to support them as they struggle to identify their personhood, their involvement in people's lives is not controlling, but supporting.

The question that arises is this: How is the respect for the dignity and freedom of the human person as created in the image of God evident in practice, especially within the church? One can question the wider church's commitment to this fundamental dignity and freedom when one witnesses the consequences of an institutional and hierarchical structure that does not name and respect the gifts and talents of all its members as contributing to the fullness of church ministry. One can also question how the church decides who can and who cannot minister in its name, and in what way, when most of its formal ministry is closed to so many, especially women. Yet the Christian tradition has a scriptural, theological, and historical foundation that calls all baptized members of the believing community to exercise their gifts within the community in the service of others.

I. What Does It Mean to Be a Human Being Made in the Image of God?

The term "anthropology" comes from the Greek word *anthropos*, which means "human being," and is the study of the origins and development of human existence. "Theological anthropology" is the reflection on the origins and development of the human person in the light of Christian belief. It does not ask simply, "What does it mean to be a human being?" but "What does it mean to be a human being who is made in the image and likeness of God?" Theological anthropology also tries to understand evil and sin within this context, and how God's grace can enter into the human situation in the face of sinfulness. In answering these questions, it looks at human existence as open to God's love and self-communication, and as related to the incarnation and redemption of Jesus.[3] Theological anthropology must also examine what has been said about human existence in the historical message of faith. Christians believe that God has been revealed to them and has spoken to them. The truth of the Christian message is revealed to us so that we do not remain hidden from ourselves. The message is that we are persons created by grace and love. We are a holy people. Long before anthropology was an academic discipline, there was an ongoing discussion about the human person in the Christian tradition. Recurring themes in this tradition are the following: the person as image of God, the person as both graced and sinful, and the conviction that these aspects of the human person unfold only within a relational and social context.

Unfortunately, when influential early Christian writers began to reflect philosophically on the human person before God, the emphasis on the relational and social aspects of being created in the image of a relational and loving God was lost. Christian life became a private affair between an individual and God. Christianity turned in upon itself and emphasized "spiritual perfection" rather than "spiritual freedom." The pursuit of individual, non-relational holiness became the dominant concern in the life of believers. Mary Garascia explains this development as follows:

> Participation in the affairs of the world was regarded as detracting from the possibility of spiritual perfection because the world was regarded as the lower story of a two-storied universe. At times this belief became outright suspicious that the secular world was hostile to the religious dimensions of the person. From this antiworld perspective, the only historical realization of the kingdom of God was the church itself and its ongoing structure.[4]

This perspective was perpetuated in the Augustinian tradition (St. Augustine, 354–430), in which an understanding of the human person was strongly connected to individual consciousness. The way the soul came to know itself, and God, was through introspection and self-reflection. There was little emphasis on the relational, social, and communal aspects of human living. This lack of relationality was further entrenched by the theology of St. Severinus Boethius (480–524), who defined the human person as an "individual substance of a rational nature." His definition solidified the individualistic understanding of person as centre of consciousness, and was extremely influential in scholastic theology.[5] This introspective heritage dominated the theology of St. Thomas Aquinas (1225–74), resulting in an abstract understanding of the human person, with the image of God located in the intellect:

> Man is called the image of God, not that he is essentially an image; but that the image of God is impressed on his mind; as a coin is an image of the king, as having the image of the king. Wherefore there is no need to consider the image of God as existing only in every part of man. (ST. I, q.93, a. 6)

> Our being bears the image of God so far as it is proper to us, and excels that of the other animals, that is to say, insofar as we are endowed with a mind. (ST, I, q. 93, a. 7)[6]

The Enlightenment, the philosophical and scientific movement of the seventeenth and eighteenth centuries, reinforced the notion of person as self-consciousness. René Descartes (1590–1650) "turned toward the subject." He proposed that the human self establishes its existence and reality by thinking: *cogito ergo sum* ("I think, therefore I am."). The person is the centre, and God exists to the extent that the human subject establishes the divine subject as another "self."[7] This understanding isolated the person from the world, and perpetuated the belief that the person can be a self by itself. As La Cugna points out, other philosophers followed suit:

> John Locke defined person in terms of self-consciousness and Leibniz thought of personhood as an enduring self-awareness that is present to itself and knows itself despite external bodily changes. Kant completed these definitions with the note of morality: A person is a self-conscious moral subject who is responsible for his or her actions.[8]

All of these philosophical principles have contributed to an anthropology as well as to a theological tradition of privatism, isolationism, and individualism.

Human personhood is much broader than the intellect alone, however, and the fullness of such a relational and social personhood cannot have the self as its primary referent. It is the person in the totality of personhood—mind, body, and soul, living within the context of historical human relational experience in the world, and responding to God's free self-communication in history—that provides the conditions for a complete theological anthropology. The source of our dignity and freedom is our potential for encountering God's grace and living the fullness of this encounter in our everyday lives.

Within the divine–human encounter, initiated by God's love, we come to know ourselves. This ability to know highlights the tremendous potential of the human person, but it comes with a responsibility. As created in the image of God, each person contains divine self-revelation, and it is because of this free act of God that personal potential and the fullness of self-realization is possible. If we do not recognize this divine self-revelation as an intimate part of our humanity, then we will never know ourselves fully, and if we do not recognize it in ourselves, then we will never recognize it in others. If we do not believe it of ourselves, then we can never believe it of others. The mystery of God dwells within us and in the expression of our being. To fail to perceive this is to fail to appreciate the inherent divine power in every human person, and the fullness of their potential as God's creation.

Made in the image of God so that we can love and be loved makes us inherently relational, because love can only be activated in personal relationships. It is, as Thomas Groome remarks, not that we become a person first, and then relate, but, rather, that we become a person only by relating. For this reason, Groome prefers the word "person" to describe us, rather than "individual," because

> [t]he latter is from 'individuare'—literally 'to stand apart'—whereas person is from the Greek 'proposon'—meaning 'turned toward the other.' The very term person bespeaks that we become human through partnership with others.[9]

One can even go so far as to say that we are saved through partnership: partnership with God and with others. There is no room for individualism in such partnerships. Personhood is not individuality. We naturally seek relationships of all kinds in family, friendships, communities, and in the wider society. In these relationships we recognize our rights and exercise our responsibilities. In living these relationships we also gradually come to understand that we are created to be respected as human beings, and that we too have a responsibility to respect others. On this mutuality of rights and responsibilities, Groome further states:

> Rights and responsibilities are two sides of the same coin of personhood. Just as we claim and exercise our rights, so we always remain responsible for promoting the rights of all. In fact, it's by fulfilling our responsibility to the 'other' that we recognize the other and realize our own personhood....We always need God's help to fulfil our responsibilities but we cannot delegate them. Responsibility and accountability are integral to being human.[10]

This renewed emphasis on the relational and social nature of the human person has been restored to prominence in Christian anthropology, and has resulted in a resurgence of the belief of the early church that we become holy through active participation in the community and in the wider society. This anthropology is an imperative of the gospel, where Christians are commanded by Jesus to "be one as [I and the Father] are one" (Jn 17:22), and to pray for the coming reign of God on earth as well as in heaven. The social dimension of the human person speaks to the obligation of people to participate in, and to transform, the social order. The image of the church as the People of God, with its scriptural and patristic roots, addresses the possibility of such a transformed social reality. What is new in current theological anthropology, however, is the emphasis that such a social reality is directly associated with the understanding of the person as created in the image of God.

When we accept each person as a reflection of the divine image, relationships within the community of the People of God are revealed as mutual rather than hierarchical. This new appreciation of the interdependence of church, society, and person leads to a dramatic reversal of the tendency toward private holiness and disdain for the world. Our faith is a social reality and it demands to be lived as such. *Gaudium et Spes* goes so far as to say that the "split between the faith which many profess and their daily lives deserves to be counted among the more serious errors of our age" (*GS* 43). Thus, faith communities are called both to nourish the inner faith life of people and to motivate them to transform the social order. They can do this by emphasizing both the communal and societal dimensions of what Garascia calls an "anthropology of interdependence."[11]

Human Dignity and Freedom in Gaudium et Spes

The dignity and freedom that is ours as creatures made in the image of God, and our salvation through Jesus Christ, is the operative principle of the theological anthropology of *Gaudium et Spes*. Three major consequences follow from this dominant image of the human person. First, as created beings we are *embodied* beings, beings with a body, a soul, and a mind; second, each person is divinely endowed with the capacity for freedom of action according to the dictates of moral conscience; and third, each person is created for interpersonal relationships. This understanding of the human person serves to critique any political, social, or institutional structure that undermines these conditions for human dignity and freedom.[12] By using the principles of embodied reality, freedom exercised in the dignity of moral conscience, and the interpersonal relationality of the human person, and situating them within particular historical contexts, *Gaudium et Spes* proposes a holistic description of the person. *Gaudium et Spes* also acknowledges that historical and cultural elements influence the dignity of the human person. Human dignity is not abstract or ahistorical; it is conditioned by unique cultural and historical epochs. This means that an understanding of the human person should appeal to historical and cultural particularity, rather than metaphysical and universal principles.

Gaudium et Spes unfolds these holistic principles in the following way: God has created our body, it is sacred and holy, and God will raise it up on the last day. The original creative intention of the sanctity of the whole person integrates the body and soul as the fruits of creation. As body and soul, and out of respect for self, and for God's creation, the human person is to regard the body as good and honourable, and not to despise or abuse bodily life in any way.

The mind is also important. It is integral to the human person and has a special dignity because it helps us in the pursuit of truth and wisdom. The intellectual nature of the human person is perfected by wisdom. Wisdom gently attracts us to a quest and a love for what is good and true (GS 14).

The pursuit of true goodness is related to the dignity of each person's moral conscience. As made in the image of God, each person is endowed with a conscience, which the Constitution describes as the "most secret core and sanctuary" of a person (*GS* 16). God has made us for God's own, and in our hearts is written the law of God. In the depths of our conscience, there is a law that we do not impose upon ourselves but that holds us to the loving obedience of God. To listen to this love, and to obey its call, is the very dignity and freedom of human personhood (*GS* 16). Conscience implies responsibility, and responsibility can only be exercised in the fullness of personal freedom. It is only in freedom that each of us can direct ourselves toward this goodness, and this freedom is directly related to our image of God: "For its part, authentic freedom is an exceptional sign of the divine image within" us (*GS* 17). Our dignity demands that we act according to a knowing and free choice. Such choice does not result from "blind internal impulse nor from mere external pressure" (*GS* 17). In other words, it is only in personal freedom, and not through any type of coercion, that one can openly pursue the opportunity for meaningful decision-making.

The responsibility of moral conscience is situated squarely in the relationship between the individual and activity within community. By our innermost nature, we are social beings, and unless we relate to others, we can neither live authentically nor develop our full potential. *Gaudium et Spes* stresses that to live the dignity and freedom that constitutes the human person we need a community that respects these, and that the dialogue that is necessary to promote them can only happen at the deeper level of interpersonal relationships. Such relationships demand mutual respect for the full spiritual dignity of each person. God's plan for each personal vocation is also attached to the nature of community. All people "are called to one and the same goal, namely God" (*GS* 24). For this reason, love of God and love of neighbour is the first and the greatest commandment, and as we seek greater unity today among believers, this truth is of paramount importance. "Indeed, the Lord Jesus, when He prayed to the Father, 'that all may be one...as we are one' (Jn 17:21-22) opened up vistas closed to human reason. For he implied a certain likeness between the union of the divine Persons, and in the union of God's sons and daughters in truth and charity" (*GS* 24). A footnote to this section of the Constitution develops this point when it makes a connection between revelation and the human condition:

> For the Christian, this Constitution probably contains no bolder invitation to theological reflection than this brief allusion to the light divine revelation sheds on the meaning of [humanity's] vocation to find human and personal fulfilment in and through society. (*GS* 24, n. 71)

The person and society are interdependent. The progress of the human person and the advance of society itself hinge on each other. The beginning and goal of all social institutions is the human person, and the human person is completely in need of social structures (*GS* 25). Thus, the social order must be structured for the benefit of the human person. Social structures and institutions are subordinate to the personal realm, and not vice versa, as Jesus indicated when he said that the sabbath was made for the human person, and not the person for the sabbath (*GS* 26).

> This social order requires constant improvement. It must be founded in truth, built on justice, and animated by love; in freedom it should grow every day toward a more humane balance. An improvement in attitudes and widespread changes in society will have to take place if these objectives are to be gained. (*GS* 26)

The essential equality of all peoples can flourish only within a social order that serves the personal realm. Every type of discrimination, whether social or cultural, whether based on sex, race, colour, or religion, is contrary to God's intent for the human person. This same dignity and freedom that God promises must also be exercised within the church, and extended to all of the faithful (*GS* 62, n. 206). The community of the church that gathers in the name of Jesus Christ is called to be a shining example of equality and unity; only in this way can it witness to the belief that every person is created in the image of God.

We are all created in the image of God and we are each unique. Our uniqueness reminds us that we are all equally valued by God. We are not interchangeable and disposable. Our uniqueness identifies who we are in relationships and in community. This uniqueness is also responsible for the personal gifts that each of us contributes to communal relationships and to the functioning of community. Paradoxically, our uniqueness is what we all have in common. In fulfilling the uniqueness of who we are, we live our birthright as sons and daughters of our loving God.

II. The Interconnectedness of Salvation and Human Freedom

Redemptive salvation and human freedom are at the centre of Christian anthropology. The principal question about personal dignity and freedom is actually a question about salvation. Salvation calls for a relationship between humanity and God. Salvation is the goal of creation: to be saved is to be fully united with God, and with one another in God. Salvation means that there is an intimate relationship between God, ourselves, and others. Personal freedom and salvation are integrally connected. The personal freedom that comes from the redemptive work of salvation in Jesus is the core of the Christian life. In connecting these two, Karl Rahner says that "the true theological notion of salvation...means...the final and definitive validity of a person's true self-understanding and true self-realization in freedom before God."[13] It is our capacity to become a partner with God in a genuine dialogue, or covenant relationship, which leads to intimacy with God. God and humanity meet as persons in communion. In creation and salvation God and humanity encounter one another in the mystery of communion and interdependence. Therefore, the model for human existence is personhood, relationship, and communion. We become who we are, and who we are meant to be, through relationships with other people and with God.

Our dignity and freedom demands realization and respect, and because it is from God, it can never be lost. While we cannot lose our dignity and freedom completely, too often we lose sight of it, or it is not nurtured in the first place. Instead, we have no sense of our own dignity and freedom, and our lives become meaningless, or hopeless. God's love and grace redeem us from such meaninglessness and hopelessness, and our dignity and freedom comes from this relationship of love and grace alone.

Since human dignity and freedom is relational, there is both a social and a historical dimension to salvation. Salvation is always worked out in history. Human existence must always be considered from both a personal and a social perspective. Yes, each person enjoys an inner autonomy, but the self is always a responding self. There is an outward actuality to the self, and our responsibility to be ourselves lies not only in self-consciousness, but in self-realization. We cannot remain hidden in an interior disposition. The authentic freedom of a genuine Christian anthropology is always mediated in the concrete and external reality of our history. Our existence involves both personal freedom and social responsibility. The more we live responsible freedom, the more we give glory to our creator God, and the more we enter into the dynamic of salvation history. Freedom means an ultimate openness; an openness to love and to truth. It is the ability to decide about oneself, and to actualize the fullness of one's potential. Freedom means that we are able to establish the unique identity of the person we are before and with God. Such freedom comes only from God's love for us, and because God's love is never coercive, we are able to decide who and what we want to be. It is this sense of freedom that moves us beyond a purely interior self out into loving relationships.

If we are going to live the fullness of our potential, then we have to love: love God, love self, and love our neighbour. We are not simply rational beings: we are spiritual, social, and relational; we are embodied; and we are free. Our human nature speaks to our dependence on God, and on our ability for self-transcendence that unites us with God, and our freedom flows from this unity. All of these are connected to our image of God, and because God is a God of love, they are all dependent upon loving relations between God, self, and others.

To Live in Freedom Is to Live in Love

"God is Love." This is the definitive description of God that we find throughout all of scripture. To say that "God is Love" is to affirm that God can only be known in relationship, because there can be no love unless there are personal relationships. God made us to be lovers; we actualize the fullest possible aspect of our humanity when we love, and when we know that we are loved. Groome speaks of this love in the following way:

> And given the divine–human partnership, God's love is the model for humanity's. So human love is not some easy romanticism or license, but requires right and loving relationships with God, self, others, and creation. Love demands justice and responsibility to the neighbour. Echoing his Hebrew faith, Jesus preached such radical love as the 'greatest commandment,' (Mk 12:31): love for God, with all one's mind, heart, and soul, and strength, and for neighbour as for oneself – including our enemies.[14]

26

To personify this love, God came to us in the person of Jesus Christ. Jesus is who God is. From our reading of scripture we learn that God wants us to establish a relationship with Jesus, and Jesus wants us to know and to love God: God wants to be our "Abba." God desires the intimacy with us that we see in the God/Jesus "Abba" relationship. Everything that Jesus did, he did as the one sent by God to love us. Jesus wants to be intimate with us. He wants to seek and to develop a personal relationship with each of us so that he can bring us to the fullness of our salvation and freedom before God. Jesus came so that we might experience the saving love of God. The unfolding of our lives is the continuous longing of Jesus to bring us into the love of God. The relationship that Jesus has with each of us is a personally defining relationship that is to be lived out in the process of our lives.

Jesus' life, death, and resurrection enacts the process of our lives. He calls us to reflect his life by loving God, and he shows us what this love of God is. In the love that Jesus reveals to us, we learn that there is an intimate connection between love, mission, and obedience. Everything that Jesus does for us is for the building up of the reign of God, and he shows us that participating in this reign is the way to the fullness of personal freedom and salvation. To follow Jesus and to imitate him is God's will for us. Jesus is God's will incarnate, and we know what God's will is when we experience God's love in Jesus. When we become aware of the presence of God in our lives, and the purpose of God's love for us, we move to a deeper knowledge of ourselves. When we come to know our deepest selves, we come to know who we are as created in the image of God. To be created in the image of God is to be created in and for love. It is in love that we find meaning in our lives, and it is in our relationship with God that we find true love. The love of God defines who we are as persons.

God's love for us, and our awareness of this love, also inspires us to love and to help others. Love is never for ourselves alone. This is particularly evident in the Risen Lord's relationship with his disciples. As God sent Jesus to bring the peace and joy of the reign of Love into the world, so Jesus sends his disciples to do the same. His message to those to whom he appeared was quite clear: Go and proclaim what you have seen and heard, and what you have experienced in your heart, and do this in the assurance that the peace and joy of the Risen Lord will be with you always (Mt 28:19-20; Mk 16:15; Jn 20:19-23). Thus, with the resurrection, the faith of those who loved Jesus and who believed in him as the Risen Lord was deepened, and with this deepening of their love came an intensity of the presence of Jesus, together with an urgency of their command to witness in the name of the Father, and of the Son, and of the Holy Spirit. It was a command that called them to be what they witnessed: the Love of God.

Just as the love that God has for Jesus is a witness to God's reign of Love, so the witness of the love of the Risen Jesus is, for us, a call to be witnesses to this reign. Jesus taught us what it means to live for the reign of Love: anyone who loses his or her life for Jesus' sake will find it. To lose our life for Jesus' sake means to give our lives for the work of God's reign. When we work for the reign of God, we are doing what God wishes for us. When we do what God wants us to do, we are fulfilling the deep potential for which God created us: the call to loving discipleship.

What Happens When We Ignore the Human Freedom to Love?

When we ignore this love and our freedom for goodness, we resort to sinfulness. Thus, while created in the image of God, the human person is also marked by sin. From the beginning of history, humanity has ignored or misunderstood this freedom by breaking the bonds between God, self, and others, and with all of creation. Sin diminishes humanity and blocks its path to fulfillment, and the opportunity for each person to attain their full potential. For whatever reason, we do not always accept the gracious love of God, and a rejection of this love in freedom has devastating effects on what we think of ourselves, and others. McBrien comments on some instances that arise from this:

> For example, if I think of myself as utterly without worth, I am saying something about the divine estimation of God's own handiwork, about the effectiveness of Jesus Christ's redemptive work on my behalf, and about the value of being a member of the church, and of having access to the sacraments, about the meaningfulness of my life as a Christian, and about the basis of our common hope in the coming of God's kingdom.[15]

There are many instances in our lives when we allow God's love for us to be eclipsed. In describing the human condition, therefore, we must also recognize our capacity for sin. We originate with sinful tendencies, and it is not only our personal lives but also our social structures that reflect this tendency. To refuse to love, to refuse to enter into loving relationships, is the basis of sin. When we refuse to love others, and to enter into full relationship with them, we refuse to recognize them as created in the image of God. To refuse to recognize God in one of God's creatures, including ourselves, is to refuse to recognize God. The reality of sin thus raises a stumbling block for our description of the human person as created in God's image.

If we are created in God's image, and God is not capable of sin, then why do we sin? An obvious answer is that, while we are images of God, we are not God. The reality of sin also raises the question of whether we are inherently evil and inevitably choose sin. This is not the belief of our Christian tradition. The Christian tradition teaches us that the human person is essentially good, and with the help of God's grace, is capable of free choice. While sin is part of our human nature, it does not define us. Our God has created us for love, and this is what defines us. Christians also believe that by his life, death, and resurrection, Jesus broke the hold that sin had on people, and renewed the capacity for goodness. Jesus transformed the human condition and restored us as sons and daughters of God (Gal 4:5-6). Through Jesus, the defining orientation of the human person is for the good, and for God.

Many aspects of our personal lives and the social reality in which we live prevent us from listening to Jesus' invitation to intimacy. Yet this intimate relationship brings meaning to our lives as Christians, and allows us to live the full potential of who we are. Many things also separate us from the love of God, both on a personal and a social level, and turn us inward to rely on our own resources. Getting in touch with those elements in our lives that cut us off from a deeper intimacy with Jesus will help us to uncover those parts of our lives that are overshadowed by sinfulness. God created us to love and to be able to express our gratitude for this love. Anything that hinders this love in any way is not of God. It is only when these hindrances are removed that we can enter into the freedom of relationship that God wants for us. Often it is a struggle to remove these hindrances, and in many instances they can leave us vulnerable and overcome by the darkness of sin. As Paul tells us:

> For we know that the law is spiritual; but I am of the flesh, sold into slavery to sin. I do not understand my own actions. For I do not do what I want, but I do the very thing I hate.... For I do not do the good I want, but the evil I do not want is what I do.

29

Now if I do what I do not want, it is no longer I that do it, but sin that dwells within me. (Rom 7:14-20)

We can break this cycle of sin by being open to God's grace. We know from the resurrection of Jesus that sin is not the answer to the meaning of our lives. There is nothing that God will not do for those God loves and who believe, and this has been shown most of all in Jesus being raised from the dead to new life. God sent Jesus to us, and brought him back to us. We will never lose Jesus again—this is God's promise to us. As the Risen Lord, Jesus brought a new sense of love and joy to those who knew and loved him. In his life, death, and resurrection, he was able to show the triumphant glory of the love that God has for each of us. In his joy, he can bring new-found joy to others, and what he has accomplished is poured out into our lives. Thus, we, too, will be able to bring a new sense of joy to those we know, especially to those to whom we minister, because Jesus has shared with us the triumphant glory of the love that God shared with him. This new joy also helps us to overcome the evil in our lives, just as it overcame the evil and suffering in Jesus' life. We can be joyful in knowing how much Jesus loves us, and, through him, how much we are loved by God.

This joy is blocked when we fail to see in ourselves, and in others, the reality that we are all potential vehicles of divine self-communication. Yet this potential grounds our shared human dignity and freedom, and if we do not acknowledge it, then we fail to love and serve our neighbour as God does. To fail to love and serve our neighbour is, ultimately, a rejection of the love of God. How we treat our neighbour reveals what we believe about ourselves, and what we believe about God. Our condemnation and rejection of others is really a condemnation and rejection of ourselves. To love one's neighbour is to show our love for God, and to activate our potential as God's created beings. Love is active and relational. It is impossible to love in the abstract, that is, in an intellectual and introspective way. Consequently, since God's way of relating to us is to love us, and since we are created in God's image, then, we, too, are called to relate to others in love. The underdeveloped philosophical, or metaphysical, idea of the human person falls short of such outward expression of the divine–human relationship between God and humanity active in love.

Christian anthropology, when fully understood and enacted, has a compelling vision of humanity. In describing the human person in reference to God, it grants every person dignity, freedom, capabilities, and responsibilities, all of which are grounded God's creative action. The Christian doctrines that state that everyone reflects the divine image, and that God became a human person like us in Jesus Christ, explicate an awesome reality with incredibly rich implications for each of us. These accounts of creation and incarnation reflect that, first, we share the very life of God, and second, that God shares our human life in Jesus. This is the affirmation of the human condition, and it applies to all people without exception.

Groome captures the intensity of this when he says: "No one is any more made in the image of God than anyone else. Before God we are all equal by birthright."[16] Yes, we are capable of sin, and, yes, we have an inclination to sin, but as created in God's image, and as redeemed by the life, death, and resurrection of Jesus, we are graced, rather than sinful. In the Incarnation, Jesus came to free and to strengthen humanity by renewing all peoples and casting out the darkness of evil that held humanity in the grip of sin.

This is perhaps one of the most crucial elements of ministry: whether we believe that people are graced, or sinful, will determine how we minister to them.

Retrieving "Image of God" as the Basis of Human Personhood

Retrieving the dignity and freedom of the human person as created in the image of God is essential to the operative principle of theological anthropology, and is, ultimately, bound to our way of being church. The centrality of the person as image of God is grounded in, and is inseparable from, the Christian doctrines of revelation and christology, and the dynamics of person as relational and community-forming find their source in the Trinity. This process of revelation, christology, and Trinity will be unfolded in the next three chapters.

To understand the person as image of God—that is, a human person imbued with the divine—is an incredible thing. It indicates God's unique and ultimate relationship with humanity, and the desire of God to seek a personal union with each person. God's desire is actualized in the doctrine of the Incarnation, and our christology shows that in becoming human in the person of Jesus Christ, God confirms the dignity of the human person. In the Trinity, we are reminded that Jesus gives us his Spirit, and remains not simply with us, but within us, and that the communion and unity of the Father, Son, and Holy Spirit is the goal of each person. The implications of the person as image of God, as described in a theological anthropology grounded in the doctrines of revelation, christology, and trinity, find their expression in the sacramental life of the believing community as it gathers and ministers as church. These doctrines, together with a theology of sacrament and church, highlight the uniqueness of the divine–human relationship, and provide a theological framework for the definitive features of the human person. Our theological statements about God, Jesus, the Trinity, the sacraments, and the church are always a reflection of our understanding of human existence and the human condition.

It is only in the church, *as a community*, that the uniqueness of each person, and the diversity of their gifts, can be welcomed and celebrated. The human person cannot live the fullness of relationship without community. We cannot actualize ourselves outside relationships. The purpose of community is to nourish the well-being of people so that they can reach their full relational potential. The church community is, therefore, called to be a community of service that incorporates a variety of charisms and ministries into its functioning, and is welcoming to all. As David Power points out, such a church

> would give primacy to the mission to service God's reign in society and would spell this out in terms of service to the poor and oppressed and a struggle for a just society. Its common life would be marked by simplicity, poverty, and non-discrimination. Its service would derive from charisms, spiritual authority, and competency, and it would make use of the criterion of discernment of spirits in the ritual and official ordering of its ministry. The paradigm of order would be organic, not hierarchical. Institutional needs are not ignored in this paradigm, but ministry is not confined to office-holders.[17]

The witness of the church community links revelation and human experience in a way that is decisive for how we live our faith and how we minister. The necessity of an interdependent community shows that an individualistic or authoritarian understanding and expression of Christianity is impossible. Community witnesses to the reality that the life of a Christian is marked by hospitality and service. The church as a corporate personality is identified as the People of God and the Body of Christ, and precisely because we are all the People of God and part of the Body of Christ, there is an interrelationship between, and an interdependence upon, every member of the church community. We are all equal members of the church, and an interdependent church structure would reflect this. Only interdependence and unity, and not institution and hierarchy, can mirror the loving action of God. The way we live in community reveals what we believe about the human person, and what we believe our Christian mission to be.

Chapter 2

Revelation: God for Us

Whoever has seen me has seen the Father.... The words that I say to you I do not speak on my own; but the Father who dwells in me does his works. (Jn 14:9-10)

Introduction

Revelation is the Word of God, as the expression of the Father, in the Son, through the Holy Spirit.[1] Everything we say about revelation must refer to this singular source. In the Word, God is revealed to us as the Creator and Lord of human history, and becomes incarnate in the person of Jesus Christ. Jesus is the self-revelatory Word of God active through the whole of creation: "In the beginning was the Word, and the Word was with God, and the Word was God.... All things came into being through him, and without him not one thing came into being" (Jn 1:1, 3). Jesus is also the reference by which we understand and interpret the revealed Word of God in scripture. Jesus continued his disclosure as the Word in sending the Holy Spirit to help us to understand it more fully. This specifically Christian way of speaking about God's revelation is trinitarian: God, Jesus, and the Holy Spirit. The structure of revelation in Word and Spirit asserts God's trinitarian nature.

The continued work of the Holy Spirit in the world shows that revelation is an ongoing process. We continue to grapple with the meaning of the Word of God disclosed in the life, death, and resurrection of Jesus as revealed to us in scripture. When we seek to understand and interpret the meanings and values of Jesus' life for us today, we are engaging in the theological task of "hermeneutics," which is the interpretation of the

Word of God in the Christian tradition. The meanings and values of Jesus' life, death, and resurrection that we uncover and transmit are about the person of Jesus himself, and what he passed on to his disciples. Recovering and transmitting these meanings and values is continued through the inspiration of the Holy Spirit.[2]

To affirm revelation as the self-disclosed word of God is to restate the basic Christian doctrine that God has spoken to us. God has initiated a personal dialogue with us: we are invited to listen and to respond. God's words are God's revelation to us, and our response is faith.

Faith is the correlative of revelation. Revelation becomes actual only when it is accepted in faith by each believer. Until we accept God's self-communication in our personal faith life, revelation is nothing more than potential for us.[3]

The interdependence of revelation and faith parallels the interpersonal relationship between God and humanity. Revelation is not simply a set of doctrinal propositions, and faith is not simply a matter of giving intellectual assent to a set of belief statements about God. Rather, our God is a personal God who comes to us in grace and love in the person of Jesus Christ. The Incarnation has far-reaching implications for our understanding of revelation. Revelation is the concrete reality of a human person, not some abstract theological theory. Revelation is interpersonal, not propositional. It is part of our embodied history, and not an idealistic philosophical principle.[4]

These distinctions in revelation are often contrasted between an intellectual model, where faith is defined as the intellectual assent to divinely revealed truths contained in church doctrine. and a personalist model, where faith is defined as a total personal commitment to the love of God revealed in Jesus Christ.[5] But understanding revelation as God seeking a personal relationship with each of us in the person of Jesus Christ compromises neither traditional church doctrine nor personal faith experience. Contemporary theology defines faith in the revealed Word of God in personalist terms, but this does not concede the fundamental truth of the doctrine of revelation that Christian doctrine claims. The task of systematic theology is to understand the church's doctrines, and to express their meanings in ways that are appropriate for our contemporary situation. The personalist model of revelation is one that relates well to this context.

I. In the Context of Our Lives God Is for Us

God relates to us and speaks to us in the natural world of creation. Revelation is certainly God's initiative, but it can become a reality for us only within the context of our lives. God is revealed to us through the things and events that we perceive in our everyday experience, which are our only links to the mysteries of our belief. To describe God in human terms is always inadequate, but we have no other way of talking about the mystery of God's revelation to us. Some questions arise from this: How can we recognize the Word of God in scripture as the Word of God without reducing it to a merely human word? How can a finite person know and experience God? How can we know about the inner reality of our faith?

Our search for the answers to these questions is part of the quest for meaning in our lives. It is a search for something in the human person that points beyond itself. This capacity to search for, and to realize, something beyond the limit of our selves is often referred to in Christian theology as the transcendental principle.[6] This principle can be summarized as follows: We are created by and for God. God can reveal who God is to us because, through this creation, God is already present in our lives. It is precisely because of this presence that we are capable of recognizing God's revelation. God gives us the potential to listen to and to accept God's personal disclosure and communication in faith, hope, and love.

Underlying this theological conviction is the philosophical principle that there are certain preconditions within us that allow us to know anything at all. This leads us to ask: What *a priori*, or prior, structures exist within the human person? When we relate this question to revelation, it becomes: What kind of hearer does Christianity assume so that the Word of God can be heard?[7] The answer lies in our belief that we are created by God: because we are created by and for God such self-transcendent knowing can only be understood as taking place by God. God is understood to be so intrinsic to who we are that we are empowered by God's grace to be able to achieve such real and actual transcendence.[8] While theology relies on a philosophical principle of knowing to articulate an understanding of self-transcendence, it moves beyond knowledge to the actuality of our lives. Neil Ormerod's insights are helpful in describing this movement from knowledge to reality:

[I]t is not simply that our knowledge of the Christian message conditions our knowledge of the human subject, but that the reality of the Christian message conditions the reality of the human subject, that the human subject exists with a radical orientation to God. It is this orientation or 'supernatural existential' which marks the human person out as a potential 'hearer of the word'.... It is this supernatural existential, which is already a share in God's grace or divine self-communication, which allows us to hear the Word of God, which is God, as a truly divine Word, and not reduce it to a merely human word.[9]

Our self-transcendence, then, has to do with God. We know who God is because God wants us to know. While transcendentality takes place in the material reality of our lives, it never becomes identical with our own personal history. What God relates to in our world cannot fully contain the trinitarian God because it is not God. Kathryn Tanner captures this basic theological principle succinctly when she states:

God cannot give Godself, in imitation of trinitarian relations of perfect divine communion, to what is not God, simply as such. Unlike the fully consubstantial Persons of the Trinity, creatures are not of the same essence or substance as God and therefore the Persons of the Trinity cannot communicate to creatures what they communicate to one another.... Initially at least, then, 'the diffusion that occurred in time in the creation of the world is no more than a pivot or point in comparison with the immense sweep of the divine goodness.'[10]

To think that God, in our self-transcendence, is identical with our personal history is to domesticate God in a way that can lead to idolatry. The dynamism at work in transcendentality is that of God's transcendental self-communication toward its historical realization for us, which is God's revelation, and, as such, it remains God's revelation; it does not become merely human knowledge of what revelation is. Revelation is not absorbed in human knowing, it is distinctly the living reality of God in our lives. It is God's own continued action in the world.[11]

Human History/Salvation History

In order to be revealed in the world, God chooses the way of human history; this is the centre of Christian anthropology. God intervenes in our history, and we are invited to respond. God's invitation to us is one of grace and love, and, because of our transcendental nature, we have been created with the potential to accept it. The goal of our creation is salvation, and when we enter into full relationship with God, we participate in the message of salvation. Through faith, we personally respond to God's initiative of love, and surrender our whole self to this saving grace. Since our response must be personal, we can see that revelation is both personalized and personalizing.[12] The personal characteristic of this response means that it is the sole responsibility of each one of us; no one can make it on our behalf.

This kind of revelation has the character of an event, which gives it its historical status. God reveals not simply through words, but through "…the works performed by God in the history of salvation."[13] Thus, the history of the world and the history of salvation are not distinct entities. The historical process of God's self-disclosure, beginning with creation, proceeds through the revelation made to Abraham, Moses and the prophets, and reaches its fulfillment in Jesus Christ.

The transcendental revelation of God's gift of Godself to us is always mediated—that is, made known to us—in the world. Ultimately, our history is the history of transcendentality itself, and we cannot understand our transcendentality independent of our history. If we forget this then we lose sight of who we are, and who we are called to be. Transcendentality is the condition that makes genuine history possible: when we, in our history, no longer grasp this reality, then that very history becomes blind.[14] Salvation history is about how God reaches out to us in personal and communal relationships and how we choose to respond; our history is replete with examples of how we have chosen in one way or another.

The history of salvation is history on God's part; revelation is a reality for us only because God, in grace, does the disclosing. Every statement about revelation is therefore a statement about the grace of God. In our creation, we are grounded in God's free and personal self-communication. God gives this communication freely, and we can only accept it in freedom. There is no coercion involved. Freedom constitutes us as fully responsible and authentic persons. God invites us to such personal freedom, and this divine–human relationship is the setting for the dynamic of salvation. Salvation can be summarized as the foundation of each person's authentic self-understanding and self-realization in freedom before God.[15] God always addresses us in our freedom, and we are created for freedom. Theological anthropology reminds us that such freedom is the essence of love. When God comes to us in freedom, we see God's grace at work. We can never have anything to do with God, or approach God, without being already borne by God's grace. The paradox of our creation is that in our created humanity we are radically different and distant from God as absolute mystery; yet, at the same time, because of God's grace and love, we are intimately close to this mystery.[16]

All we have to do is respond to God's love and grace in faith. Every saving act of God for us is also, and always, a saving act on our part. Saving activity without faith is impossible, and faith without an encounter with God revealing Godself is a contradiction in terms.[17] The continuous interplay of these encounters forms the nexus between history, salvation, and revelation. Our history is God's history, and our history of salvation is also the history of revelation. The history of revelation unfolds wherever the history of humanity unfolds.

Revelation is therefore both complete and ongoing. On the one hand, no new revelation is to take place until the second coming of Jesus Christ. Jesus Christ himself is the fullness of revelation. On the other hand, God is still unfolding the mystery of the grace of salvation through the events of today. The ongoing events of our graced history— that is, the participation of God in our lives—help us to understand more clearly God's revelation.

God Seeks a Personal Loving Relationship with Each of Us

We have learned throughout our salvation history that God has called us into the most intimate communion, and in our theological anthropology we saw that this is summed up in the relational proposition "God is Love" (1 Jn 4:8): "So we have known and believe the love that God has for us. God is love and those who abide in love abide in God, and God abides in them" (1 Jn 4:16). The conviction that God is a personal God is fundamental to Christian belief, and if there is one word that the Christian tradition has applied unequivocally to God it is "Love." Love produces the relationship of persons between God and humanity. God's loving choice to embrace the people of the covenant shows beyond all doubt that our God is a personal God.

To be in love is to be in love with some*one*. This is even more significant in the relationship between God and humanity. Bernard Lonergan writes:

> When someone transcendent is my beloved, he is in my heart, real to me from within me.... Since he chooses to come to me by a gift of love for him, he himself must be love.... Since loving him means loving attention to him, it is prayer, meditation, contemplation. Since love of him is fruitful, it overflows into love of all those that he loves or might love.[18]

We see expressions of this love in the Old Testament, where love constitutes the relationship between persons. Love is marked by devotion, loyalty, ultimate knowledge, and responsibility. It is not one emotion among others, but is the totality of relationship. Scripture scholar E.M. Good explains:

> In its personal character, love is closely related to the sexual realm, even when the subject is God's love; and the 'person' may be collective, as in the case of God's love for Israel as a whole. In all cases, love is the force which both initiates and maintains relationships, be it among persons or between God and [humanity].[19]

God loves extravagantly, and compassionately embraces everything that has been created (Wis 11:24; Ps 145:9). The Psalmist celebrates the whole of creation as a word of God's graciousness and goodness (Ps 136:1-9). In the activity of the chosen people, God shows special guidance in election and covenant. The very fact that God has entered into relationship with human beings in so personal a way is itself an expression of God's mercy and grace. It is a revelation of God's love. The ultimate expression of this love is that, despite the people's unfaithfulness, God refuses to turn away. Nothing can thwart God's desire for personal loving relationship. God's covenant with Israel ensures the continuance of this steadfast love (Ex 34:7; 1 Kings 3:6). God will never abandon this covenant; God's love is a faithful love, an unshakeable maintenance of the covenantal relationship.

The covenant love of God is paramount in the divine–human relationship. We are invited to love God, but our love is derived from the primary establishment of God's covenantal relationship with us. It is because God loves us that we are called to love God. In transcendental terms, God's love for humanity is the agent of humanity's love for God. God's grace motivates our love. "The great commandment: 'You shall love the Lord your God with all your heart, and with all your soul, and with all your might' (Deut 6:5; cf. 13:3), sets forth humanity's response to God, and God's sole claim to our love."[20] Throughout its history, Israel came to understand that God had only one reason to reveal Godself to them: sheer grace-filled love. The promise of the covenant is that this love will never end. In the words of the prophet Jeremiah, God declares: "I have loved you with an everlasting love; therefore, I have continued my faithfulness to you" (Jer 31:3).

The Old Testament understanding of the love of God is decisive for the New Testament understanding of love and grace. In the New Testament we see further action of God's loving desire for humanity. God wants to entrust Godself to us in transcendent identity, that is, in the inner mystery of God's own personal life.[21]

Love in the New Testament is first and foremost an action; it is a free gift of God in Jesus Christ. Love is an event. It is God's action on God's part, not simply one aspect of God's character. Love is something that God does, not something that is assigned to who God is. In the Incarnation God's inmost life is communicated to us in love for us, fully and without restraint. Rahner points out that such personal love always has two characteristics:

> Love is not the emanation of nature but the free bestowal of a person, who possesses himself, who can therefore refuse himself, whose surrender is always a wonder and a grace. And love in the fully personal sense is not just any relationship between two persons who meet in some third thing, whether this 'third thing' is a task, a truth, or anything else; it is the ceding and unfolding of one's inmost self to and for the other in love.[22]

Love is constitutive of the relationship between God and humanity. In God's loving action, and in the unfolding of God's inmost self, an intimate communion has been established. By sending God's Son, and the Spirit of Love, God has revealed God's innermost secret, the secret of who God is (1 Cor 2:7; Eph 3:9-12). God invites us into trinitarian love. God's love "is an eternal exchange of love, Father, Son, and Holy Spirit, and [God] has destined us to share in that exchange."[23] God so loved the world that God gave the only Son. What has become manifest in the Son is the Love of God (Rom 5:8), and, through the Spirit, God pours forth upon us this love for us (Rom 5:5; Gal 4:6). The Spirit leads us into the deepest intimacies of God's knowledge (Jn 15:26; 16:13; 1 Cor 2:12; 1 Jn 2:20, 27), and through the Spirit we become God's adopted children (Gal 4:4-6).[24] The Holy Spirit, bearing witness with our spirit, makes us children of God. (Rom 8:15) The Spirit of God is God's personal love realized in us. Just as we are known by, and in, this love, so are we called to know God (1 Cor 13:12).

"God is Love" is not simply an illuminating statement about the nature of God; it is the statement of personal experience in which human beings have come to know God in Jesus Christ, through the Holy Spirit. Our experience is that God has entrusted God's entire Self on us.[25]

This infinite love of God, above all else, marks the teaching of Jesus. The two great commandments—"Love of God" and "Love of neighbour" (Mk 12:30-31; Mt 22:34-40)—assume a loving and lovable God. In this regard, Jesus is heir to the Old Testament understanding of love. But Jesus goes further, addressing God as "Abba, Father,"[26] showing his deep understanding and affection for God. Jesus' emphasis on the goodness of God comes from his relationship as God's Son. We, too, are able to address God as "Abba" because we, too, are God's sons and daughters through adoption.

Jesus' teaching is resplendent with examples of this loving relationship. God cares for all creatures and for all peoples (Lk 12:22ff). The smallest sparrow does not die without God's remembrance, and the very hairs on our head are numbered (Lk 12:6-7). Jesus' statements are not poetic hyperbole: they are declarations of the intimate nature of God's love as he knew it.[27] Jesus revealed the fullest expression of this love by his life. It is manifest in his relentless work for the sake of the kingdom, and embraced in his death on the cross. In the fullness of Jesus' life for others we have seen the revelation of God, and this God is Love.

The Unique Relationship Between God and Humanity

The image and likeness of God that is central to the Christian doctrine of human nature, and that is derived from our understanding of revelation, articulates the unique relationship between God and humanity. According to biblical anthropology, the whole person—body and soul, male or female—is created in God's image to be God's partner (Gen 1:26-27). Although this reference is to actual resemblance, it is widely accepted that the writer's intention was to convey the idea of human personality in relationship to God. There is little support in the Old Testament for actual physical resemblance between God and humanity, and making any image of God is explicitly forbidden (Ex 20:4).[28]

"Image" also denotes the human capacity to know and to love God, from which humanity derives its dignity. Of all God's creatures, only the human person is able to know and love the Creator, and through this knowledge and love is able to share in God's own life. Humanity was created for this purpose. Expressing this insight, St. Catherine of Siena asks:

> What made you establish [us] in so great a dignity? Certainly the incalculable love which you have looked on your creature in yourself. You are taken with love for [us], for by love indeed you created [us], by love you have given [us] a being capable of tasting your eternal Good. (St. Catherine of Siena, Dialogue 4, 13)[29]

Imago Dei—the image of God—is the theological concept that expresses the likeness of the human person to God, and is central to Christian reflection on the human condition, the meaning of redemption in Christ, and an understanding of hope for humanity.[30]

The human person in the "image of God" has dignity, not as some*thing*, but as some*one*. This dignity makes us capable of self-knowledge and self-possession, and gives us the ability to enter freely into relationship and communion with others. Even after sin, humanity still remains in the image of God (Gen 9:6) because each person can still be called, and God continues to call them. The Old Testament never suggests that the image of God was lost by the Fall. Every individual is called by grace into a covenant relationship with God, and our response of faith and love is to reciprocate this offer.

For Christians, the consummate image of God is plainly Jesus Christ (2 Cor 4:4ff; Heb 1:3). As the Son of God, Jesus portrays the Father, and as the Incarnate God, he makes God visible. The fullness of God's glory is in him. We, too, can share in this glory. Paul tells us that, by the power of the Holy Spirit, whoever believes in the Son can share in his glory and, even in this world, can become the image of the transformed Lord.[31] In the New Testament, therefore, the image of God does not belong to humanity, but is identified with Jesus Christ, and it is through a relationship with him that the Christian believer reflects this image.

Paul relates being in the image of God to humanity's destiny. He is concerned about the pastoral consequences of the belief that Christ, the beloved Son, is the image of the invisible God (Col 1:15) and with Christ being the likeness of God (2 Cor 4:4). Paul is convinced that, in relationship with Jesus Christ, humanity can attain the likeness of God.[32] He is also convinced that such a relationship can work itself out in the interrelationships that exist within the Christian community. In Colossians 3:11, Paul states that the believer's transformation in the image of the Creator will bring about a community in which racial, religious, and social distinctions will no longer have any meaning. Porteous summarizes Paul's understanding of image of God very well when he says:

> Above all, Christians must 'put on love, which binds everything together in perfect harmony.' (Col 3:14) It is in God's plan for [all] that they should 'be conformed...to the image of [God's] Son,' (Rom 8:29) and, therefore, since there is no distinction, to the image of God. This is an eschatological hope, but it is also in some real measure a present reality, for 'we all, with unveiled face, beholding the glory of the Lord, are being changed into his likeness from one degree of glory to another, for this comes from the Lord, who is the Spirit.' (2 Cor 3:18; cf. Phil 3:20-21)[33]

Following scripture, Christian anthropology continues to grapple with the statement that maintains that the human being is made in the image of God. Anthropologically, it defines the human person as open by nature to God's self-communication, and, second, this nature itself is open to the grace of Christ.[34]

The "image of God" is an evocative phrase, and has been interpreted in different ways in the history of Christian anthropology. Early theologians presented a variety of views on what they conceived "image" to mean. Some saw it as the human intellect, or the capacity for moral decision-making, while others saw it in humanity's ability to rule over creation.

The understanding of the image of God as residing in the human intellectual capacity to reason dominated the philosophical tradition from Augustine to the Enlightenment. Human rationality was understood as humanity's participation in, and reflection of, the divine *logos*, or reason, by which the world was created. However, while this estimation of human reason is somewhat justified, it fosters an intellectualization of Christian anthropology. If the essence of the human person is seen, above all else, in the process of abstract reasoning, then the emotional and physical dimensions of human existence are devalued.[35]

"Image" viewed as humanity's ability to rule over creation does not fare much better. In this interpretation, humanity resembles God in its capacity to exercise power and dominion over the earth and other creatures. In the resulting world view, in which all relationships are ordered in hierarchical patterns, "God rules over the world; the soul controls the body; men are masters of women; and humanity dominates other creatures."[36] This interpretation of image of God has often been used to legitimize the exploitation of peoples, other creatures, and nature. It has also spawned patriarchy, racism, and colonialism. Fortunately, these views are tempered with the rightly understood interpretations that the dominion that is entrusted to humanity is the same as God's, one that involves love, care, and respect for all creatures and creation, rather than mastery and manipulation.[37]

In line with scripture, however, most early theologians consented that image of God implied, above all, a relationship between God and humanity, and a personal call and response for the imitation of God in Christ. Jesus is the visible manifestation of the image according to which humanity was created, and Jesus mediates the likeness of God, both in creation and in redemption.[38] The majority of contemporary theologians support this consensus. Image of God describes human life in relationship with God and with creation. God created humankind in God's own image, male and female God created them. To be fully human is to live in relationships of mutual support and love. Humanity living in relationship reflects the life of God, who also lives eternally in relationship, and in trinitarian community. Human life in relationship, as created in the image of God, corresponds to God's own life in relationship as exemplified in Jesus Christ. Thus, in the light of the history of Jesus Christ, Christian faith and theology are led to

> interpret *imago Dei* as an *imago Christi*, and *imago trinitatis*. Just as the Incarnate Lord lived in utmost solidarity with sinners and the poor, and just as the eternal life of God is a triune society, so humanity in its coexistence with others is intended to be a creaturely reflection of the living God.[39]

45

II. Living as Image of God

...human beings as the imago Dei, *those with the greatest potential for responding as beloved to lover, can be revelatory of the God-world relationship in a special way.*[40]

Imago Dei defines the human person. This has tremendous implications for ministry, in the sense of both how we live our own image of God, and how we minister to others also created in the image of God.

We have seen that our God is a personal God who has spoken to us and who wants a personal relationship with each of us. God has entered into the heart of our experience. God is in everything that we do, is in the very materiality of our lives. Each one of us, in our transcendentality, exists with a radical orientation toward God. If we forget God's relationship to us then our lives become meaningless.

We have also seen the overwhelming indulgence of God. God wants nothing more than to love us. God wants to freely disclose God's innermost self to us and to reveal the intensity of who God is. This is what love is; this is what love does. There are no conditions on this love, God does not hold anything back from us.

If we are created in the image of God then we, too, are called to love in this way, particularly in our ministry. The God in whose image we are created is a God of love, of deep personal relationship. Love and relationship are central to what it means to be fully human, and are also central to reflection on the human condition, to the meaning of salvation, and to an understanding of hope for humanity. To be fully human is to live in relationships of mutual support and love. For Christians, it is only in relationship with Jesus Christ that we can attain this likeness to God. In the light of this central belief of theological anthropology, there are some questions that we need to ask ourselves as ministers: Do we live as image of God? Are our lives reflections of the living God? Are we living images of God?

God Wants Our Personal Freedom

Our creation as image of God means that we are freely addressed by God in love, and we have the personal freedom either to accept this love or to reject it. There is never any coercion in a loving relationship, so being created in the image of God means that we are created for freedom.

We must not, however, overlook the fact that we are creatures. Being created means that we are embodied. This is doubly affirmed for us in the Incarnation of Jesus: The Word made Flesh, and through whom we have the promised hope of the resurrection of the body. We are placed in a material world; we are embedded in a social and historical reality. Particular cultures and historical eras help to shape our identity and help us develop as fully human beings. Migliore writes:

> To a far greater extent than other animals…human beings exist
> 'exocentrically': they are drawn outside themselves by the objects
> of their experience and especially by their relations with other
> human beings. According to Wolfhart Pannenberg, 'the concept
> of self-transcendence—like the concept of openness to the world
> which is to a great extent its equivalent—summarizes a broad
> consensus among contemporary anthropologists in their effort
> to define the special character of the human.[41]

While we are born into particular situations, we can change these situations. In fact, it is often necessary in living our image of God to reassess ourselves as persons, and as communities, in our relationship with our world. Our embodiment in culture and history is affirmation of the goodness of all life as created by God; this means that we are often called to make choices for others. We make these choices in realizing the equality of every individual as also created in the image of God. In order to be able truly to reflect our God, we can only find our true identity in coexistence with each other in community, and with the rest of creation. Human existence is not individualistic, but communal, and we maintain our full humanity in the constant interplay between personal identity and communal participation. We can only exercise our freedom in continuous interaction, not in isolation.[42]

To be fully human and to live in community are inseparable, and to live in community is to live the realization of our equality with others. The French philosopher, the Marquis de Condorcet (1745–1794) said, "Either no individual of the human race has genuine rights or else all have the same; and he [or she] who votes against the right of another, whatever the religion, colour, or sex of that other, has henceforth abjured his [or her] own."[43] Human beings were created as God's partners in order to live in partnership. The first creation story makes no mention of hierarchical relationships. We are told that male and female together constitute the image of God. The implication is that human beings are to live together in mutual love, and, in the light of the New Testament, in mutual service: "There is no longer Jew or Greek, there is no longer slave or free, there is no longer male or female; for all of you are one in Christ Jesus." (Gal 3:28). We are all equal before God.

Living such equality draws human beings out beyond themselves. As image of God in self-transcendence, human persons seek a meaning and purpose in their lives that takes them beyond the individuality of their own being. The meaning that they seek often leads to the promise of a fulfilled future, and is connected to Christian hope, a hope that has been made real in the life and kingdom work of Jesus Christ.

Our relationship to the future and our hope for the fulfillment of the reign of God involves life choices. We are free to enter into partnership with God, and to work for the justice and peace that only God's reign can bring. Jesus has shown us how to do this. He glorifies God in his life and so points to the destiny of humanity: we, too, are created and redeemed to glorify God, and to work for God's reign. The structure of our lives means responsibility before God by living lives of loving, supportive relationships with others, and hopeful openness to God's promises.

Created for Loving Relationships

Love is the most intimate of all human relationships. It is integral to our lives. It brings us the most joy and the most pain. Love also contains the most potential for our development as human beings. Jean Vanier has mentioned many times in public addresses that the deepest need and want of every human being is to be loved. We all want to be loved, and to know that we are lovable.

Sallie McFague observes that we are accustomed to using the expression "God is Love," but we also know that God's love is manifested in action. If love is an action, and God expresses this love, then it makes sense to refer to God as lover, but we seldom do this: "We speak of God as love but are afraid to call God lover."[44] We are slow to use the expression mainly because of the sexual overtones that it can imply, but sexuality is only one aspect of love. To recognize God as lover brings us deeper into the reality of who God is for us. "God is Love" is an event that draws us into the intimacy of relationship. Living our lives with God as our lover activates the dynamism that is the divine createdness of who we are.

To be loved is to be found valuable. Lovers find the beloved valuable simply because the beloved is who they are; to be found valuable in this way is one of the most complete affirmations possible. To be a lover also means bringing an element of passion into a relationship. McFague notes that "passion" has two distinct meanings; although one includes sexual desire, neither of them is limited to sexual desire. Passion can mean suffering, but it also means hope, fear, love, joy, grief, and desire. She states that:

> It is perhaps no coincidence that the passion of Jesus of Nazareth has carried both of these motifs: his suffering has not been seen as passive, indifferent endurance but as agony brought on by great love toward those who need love most: the last and the least. The bond between the two meanings of passion emerges in the story of Jesus of Nazareth, whose deep feeling for those who believed themselves to be without value brought on his suffering with and for them. Disciples who model themselves on God the lover will inevitably find the same connection to obtain.[45]

Jesus' passion, death and resurrection is the fullest expression of the love of God, and the promise of new life that he offers us is the fulfillment of the loving and merciful relationship between God and humanity.

God's saving love signifies that the world is valuable, and, as created in the image of God, we are called to participate in this saving action. Salvation is not something that is performed on our behalf, but something we participate in. While this saving activity is God's initiative, it cannot be accomplished without our response. A close relationship exists between salvation and ethics: "We are made whole only as we participate in making whole."[46]

We do not always freely participate in this saving action, however, and we must ask ourselves: What stops us from being who and what we were created for? Why are we often afraid to enter into the loving partnership that God extends to us? The opposite of love is fear. What, then, can take us from fear to love? The key that opens this life of love for us is *trust*. God does not coerce us into love, but we do need to trust God. If love is the innermost part of ourselves, then we must trust ourselves because in the core of our being God's Spirit guides us.

Such trust does not come easily to us, however. Previous theological anthropology, reflecting on fallen human nature and inherited original sin, determined that the self was not to be trusted. Human nature as fallen was overemphasized at the expense of the human person as created in the image of God. Unable to trust the inner self, we needed to look outside of ourselves for guidelines, but it is the innermost part of the self that is the reflection of our loving God.

One of Paul's prayers for us speaks to this when he prays that God's love may take deeper root in our hearts: "I pray that according to the riches of [God's] glory, [God] may grant that you may be strengthened in your inner being with power through [the] Spirit, and that Christ may dwell in your hearts through faith, as you are being rooted and grounded in love" (Eph 3:16-17). It was for this that we were created.

Refusing Loving Relationships

Theological anthropology is aware that many of us, for one reason or another, or at different stages in our lives, refuse to live in partnership with God and with others. We rupture the covenant relationship and are given over to disruption, conflict, alienation, and many forms of oppression. The image of God in which humanity is created is obscured and distorted by sinfulness. McFague defines sin within the context of interpersonal relationships:

> Sin is the turning-away not from transcendent power but from interdependence with all other beings, including the matrix of being from which all life comes. It is not pride or unbelief but the refusal of relationship—the refusal to be the beloved of our lover God and the refusal to be lover of all God loves. It is the retention of hierarchies, dualisms, and outcasts so as to retain the superiority of the Self.[47]

Sin is a denial of relationships, a refusal to enter into full relationship with God, others, and creation. When we refuse relationship we deny our dependence on God, other people, and the world itself. If life in the image of God is the free acceptance of God's love and grace, then sin is the denial of our relatedness to God and the refusal to acknowledge the need of this grace. When we sin we disrupt our relationship with God and deny the fullness of our personhood.

Sin can be aggressive or passive. "Judas' act of betrayal is sin in its aggressive form; the fear and cowardice of the other disciples is sin in its passive form."[48] Moreover, if we refuse to enter into loving relationships with others, then our sin can take the form of indifference to or domination of others, such that we do not relate to them as partners, or see in them the equality and dignity with which all of us were created.

The opposite of this sin of disdain for others can be personal passivity, in which individuals refuse to, or cannot, see themselves as created with the freedom and dignity that God wants for them. In these cases, self-image is low, and fear and despair, rather than love and hope, tend to be the emotions that drive the individual. In such cases, we must be careful not to blame the victim. Migliore's example is

> to heap guilt upon battered women who feel helpless or to say that the poor are poor because they are lazy....The point is that distorted interpretations of sin can help to lock victims into their victimization by undermining their will to break free.[49]

Reinterpreting the doctrine of sin through a theological anthropology grounded in the image of God means emphasizing the dignity and destiny of each human being as resting on the belief that we are all created by God in and for love.

Being created in the image of God also means that we are called to see in others the value that God sees in them. Even after sin, we are still called by God; we are still, and always will be, valuable to God. Genuine love endures, it is faithful throughout all difficulties, and finds the beloved valuable even when others might not. Enduring love must be differentiated, however, from love that continues despite perceiving the other as worthless or sinful. Enduring love persists because the other is seen as worthy and desirable, regardless of whatever negative qualities they might have.[50]

Unfortunately, reaching out to others in love and hope can sometimes lead us either to resignation in our abilities to help them, or to presumption. These existential attitudes undermine both our ability in the face of injustice, and our ability to bring about change in working for the reign of God. We become resigned to cynicism, unable to accept the value of any measures we can take, however small. The effect is to deny our destiny as created in God's image, and as heirs to God's promises. The opposite of this is to presume that, as long as we are in control of situations, we do not need God; we can do it on our own. Eventually we become burned out and discouraged when we do not get the desired results. If we rely, instead, on the strength and grace of God, then we realize that whatever our accomplishments or failures, they are carried out with trust in God.

Our cultural context, however, tends to favour self-reliance by emphasizing external performance and success and by being results-oriented. We are conditioned to be self-centred and individualistic, and to believe that happiness and peace of mind are proportionate to individual achievement and material wealth. Competitive individualism does not serve God or others. Love and service for others are influenced by the Holy Spirit; self-centredness is not. Richard Hauser cautions:

> Unreflectively, we ministers can put ourselves at the centre of our ministry and see our ministry basically as a means of serving our kingdom rather than [God's] kingdom. We must continually challenge cultural assumptions and call ourselves back to the teachings of the Gospel.[51]

Ministering as Image of God

Ministry cannot be self-serving. Ministry is a public service grounded in the gospel and performed on behalf of the Christian community for the promotion of the reign of God. Our understanding of ministry is directly related to our understanding of God. Whether we believe that God is eternally distant or the innermost core of our being will have a tremendous effect on how we minister. Whether or not we believe that we are lovable, and can be loving in return, will determine how we practise our ministry.

Ministry has everything to do with the love of God, love of self, and love of neighbour. It is always other-centred. When we live love, we live in God, and in the Spirit sent by God, and if image of God means a life of self-value, mutual relations, and care for the world, then these qualities brought together are the mark of ministry. We are most alive, and minister most effectively, when we acknowledge our equality and solidarity with others, and with creation itself. Self-centredness has no place in ministry. To really love and minister as image of God results in "love-centred" ministry. Love must be the core of everything we are and do, if we are ministering in Jesus' name. McBrien makes this point clear when he paraphrases Paul's exhortation on love:

If love is the soul of Christian existence, it must be at the heart of every other Christian virtue. Thus, for example, *justice* without love is legalism; *faith* without love is ideology; *hope* without love is self-centredness; *forgiveness* without love is self-abasement; *fortitude* without love is recklessness; *generosity* without love is extravagance; *care* without love is mere duty; *fidelity* without love is servitude. Every virtue is an expression of love. (1 Cor 13)[52]

For Paul, love was intimate union with Christ, and he manifested this love in his ministry. He did not minister to his communities in a detached manner, but became intimately involved in the lives of the people he served, and expected no reward except that of being able to offer his love to others (1 Cor 9:18; Phil 2:17). He had experienced the overwhelming love of Christ in his radical conversion, and his perspective on life changed. All he could do was respond to this love by loving God and others with a love that was its own reward.

Paul knew that there was a cost to his ministry, which he relates to participation in the cross of Christ; but he also knew that the cross was not the end. As Jude Winkler points out, "Like Christ, Paul was attempting to transform what had previously been a source of alienation into a means of union: union with God and union with those for whose sake he was suffering."[53] He realized that ministry in the reign of God is other-centred to the point of total surrender.

Jesus was Paul's primary example for his ministry, as he is for us. Jesus speaks of his ministry as the good news of the dawning of the reign of God. His whole being and his ministry are defined by his total trust in God, who is the one who commissions him and empowers him. In this trust, he is fully responsive to the will of God and to the needs of others. He reaches out in a special way to those who are alienated from society; he is the human-being-for-others who lives in solidarity with those whom society defines as outside the social or religious structure.

The defining characteristic of Jesus' ministry is service. This is a requirement for anyone who wants to minister in his name, as Winkler says:

The disciple is to serve those who cannot repay one's activities through the prestige that one might gain by association with them. (Mk 9:30f) One is to minister to them through the power of God and not through one's own power. (Mk 9:14ff) This is possible only if one surrenders oneself into the hands of God and places one's entire trust in the Lord. (Mk 4:10ff; 10:17ff)[54]

The ministry of Jesus can be summarized as revealing the love of God to humanity. Those who minister in his name are also mandated to share the revelation that they have received, the revelation that they are created in the image of a loving God.

Jesus is more than just an example for our ministry, however. He is its very source:

"Abide in me as I abide in you. Just as the branch cannot bear fruit by itself unless it abides in the vine, neither can you unless you abide in me. I am the vine, you are the branches. Those who abide in me and I in them bear much fruit, because apart from me you can do nothing" (Jn 15:4–5).

He asks us not simply to remain *with* him, but to remain *in* him, in a relationship of total union in ministry.

Chapter 3

Christology: God–Among–Us

In those days Jesus came from Nazareth of Galilee and was baptized by John in the Jordan. And just as he was coming up out of the water, he saw the heavens torn apart and the Spirit descending like a dove on him. And a voice came from heaven, "You are my Son, the Beloved; with you I am well pleased." (Mk 1:9-11)

Introduction

Christology is the branch of systematic theology that asks such questions as these: Who is Jesus? Why is he believed to be the Messiah? What does he do for the salvation of humanity? This chapter will look at the main features of christology and how they are related to theological anthropology. It will also establish that Christian discipleship— that is, the imitation of Jesus Christ—is the foundation for all forms of ministry. A theological reflection on the Incarnation uncovers an essential relationship between christology, theological anthropology, and ministry. The Incarnation is the self-revelation of the Word of God in the world. In the Incarnation, Jesus, in the fullness of his humanity, makes God visible to us. He is the consummate "image" of God. If we are created in the image of God, and if we are called to live out our lives as this image, then we need to develop a deep understanding of who Jesus is, because we are called to imitate his life.

There is an intimate connection between Jesus and humanity, and between Jesus' humanity and our humanity. Christology and theological anthropology are mutually dependent. Christology is the beginning and the end of theological anthropology, and determines our understanding of God in theology. Rahner writes:

[T]his anthropology in its most radical actualization is for all eternity theology. It is first of all the theology which God himself has spoken by uttering his word as our flesh into the emptiness of what is not God and is even sinful, and secondly, it is the theology which we ourselves do in faith when we do not think that we could find Christ by going around man, and hence find God by going around the human altogether. But we have to say of the God whom we profess in Christ that he is exactly where we are and only there is to be found.[1]

I.   Who Is Jesus?

The christological question "Who is Jesus?" is always related to the question "Why did he come?" In theological terms, the question of Jesus' role in salvation is called the "soteriological question." Soteriology focuses on the passion, death, and resurrection of Jesus insofar as it brings about our salvation. We cannot draw a sharp distinction between christology and soteriology, however, because this would create an artificial separation between who Jesus is and what he does. Jesus brings about the reconciliation between God and humanity. *What* he does emanates from *who* he is, and *who* he is determines *what* he does.

There are other distinctions in christology that can create similar artificial separations. One is between what is called a "high" christology, which emphasizes Jesus' divinity, and a "low" christology, which emphasizes Jesus' humanity. Another distinction is often made between a christology "from below" or an "ascending" christology, and a christology "from above" or a "descending" christology. A christology "from below" begins with the humanity of Jesus and then moves toward his resurrection and his relationship with God. A christology "from above" begins with the mystery of God's self-disclosure in creation and history, and then moves to an understanding of Jesus as the Incarnate Word of God, his ministry, and his passion, death, and resurrection.[2]

Most contemporary christologies begin "from below" and take humanity, creation, or history, or a combination of these, as their starting point. Their core questions are these: What does it mean to say that a particular person is God-among-us? How could a particular person even be such recognizable as such? The challenge for Christologies "from below" is to safeguard the full humanity of Jesus while still recognizing that within this humanity Our Lord and Our God is present among us. On the other hand, a christology "from above" that overemphasizes Jesus' divinity denies the basic assertion that he identified himself fully with the human condition.[3] The challenge for any contemporary christology is to maintain the balance between the humanity and the divinity of Jesus.

If we cannot overemphasize the human or the divine in Jesus, neither can we overemphasize an ascending or a descending christology. As Rahner states: "...ascending christology and descending christology appear somewhat intermingled. It need not be a disadvantage, but rather it can serve as a mutual clarification of both these aspects and both of these methods."[4] Rahner advocates an "ascending" christology because his point of departure is our encounter with the historical Jesus "from below." However, he also advocates a "descending" christology because the Jesus we meet is the Incarnate Word of God who has broken into our history "from above": God-among-us. A focus on the Incarnation can provide us with the necessary balance between Jesus' humanity and his divinity, and can also encompass a christology "from below" and a christology "from above."

The union of the divine and human natures in Jesus Christ is called the "hypostatic union." Hypostatic union is a technical term meaning that, in Jesus, a human being became the created self-expression of the Word of God, the divine person of the Logos: "In the beginning was the Word, and the Word was with God, and the Word was God....And the Word became flesh and lived among us, and we have seen his glory, the glory as of a father's son" (John 1:1, 14). In the Incarnation, we believe that a man called Jesus of Nazareth, a Jew, who appeared over two thousand years ago, is the definitive visitation of God to humanity in history.

In *The Reality of Jesus,* Dermot Lane adds that the historical experience and the theological significance of what we believe about the Incarnation are summed up in the simple formula "Jesus Christ." Unfortunately, we lose sight of this profound christological insight because we tend to use the word "Christ" as a proper name for Jesus of Nazareth. It would be more accurate to talk of "Jesus who is called the Christ," or simply "Jesus as Christ."[5] To acknowledge Jesus of Nazareth as the Christ is to acknowledge him as the Messiah. This is the declaration of Peter in Matthew's gospel: "You are the Messiah, the Son of the Living God"

(Mt 16:16). Jesus' reply to this faith statement is also an insight for us: "Blessed are you, Simon son of Jonah! For flesh and blood has not revealed this to you, but my Father in Heaven" (Mt 16:17). Jesus' words relate to the transcendental principle. It is precisely because of the prior presence of God's grace at work in his life that Peter was able to recognize the presence of God in Jesus, and so it is with us. We saw that the function of transcendence is that humanity is moving toward something higher than it is at present. Now we see that the guarantee of this self-transcendence is the hypostatic union of the human and the divine in the Incarnation, which relates us to Jesus. In theological terms, christology and theological anthropology, although distinct, are always related to each other.

Jesus and Us

> [H]uman experience is nothing else but a challenge to entrust oneself to the development of one's own Christian existence in patience, openness and fidelity, and to do this until slowly, and perhaps painfully and with failures, this life unfolds and develops into the experience of a personal relationship to Jesus.[6]

A personal relationship with Jesus is an essential part of Christian existence. Entering into such a relationship helps us to know something about who Jesus is, which also reveals a great deal about who we are. Jesus had a lot to do with humanity; one may even say that he had everything to do with humanity. The hypostatic union is a unique event, and is also an integral moment within the process by which God's grace is given to all of humanity. This does *not* mean that the human person contains the hypostatic union as such. What Jesus is in the fullness of his humanity and what we are, are the same—we call it "human nature." There is a marked difference, however. The "what" in Jesus is the *self-expression* of the Word of God. This is not the case with us. We, in our creatureliness, are expressions of the image of God. Jesus is God; we are not. There are, as Tanner says,

> two subjects here, where a human being is assumed by Christ, and not one, as when the Son of God assumed humanity rather than a man. This difference means that, unlike Christ who simply is the Word, we come to Christ from a distance, by way of an external call; addressing us, Christ appears outside us as the one to whom we are to be united. Our relation to Christ has more

the flavor, then, of Christ's own relation to the Father, a relationship of fellowship and correspondence of wills. Our will is not Christ's will in the way the human will of Christ simply is the will of the Son, without needing to be brought into correspondence with it. Instead, our lives are made over as a result of their being assumed [by Jesus].[7]

This communication to us in the fullness of humanity shows that God wants to relate to all of humankind in grace and glory.[8] The *self*-expression of God in the Incarnation means that when God becomes what God is not, God becomes a human person. This does not reduce the stature of human nature, but enacts the encounter of God with humanity. By God becoming human, the human person becomes someone who can participate in the infinite mystery of God. To help to explain this mystery we can use the analogy of the question and answer: a question participates in its answer, and the question is born only by the possibility of the answer itself. In the Incarnation of the Logos, the question of our human existence is answered historically with God in the expression of God's own self. If God in God's *self*-expression is human, then we would be thinking little of God when we think little of ourselves. Humanity is for all eternity the expression of God because Jesus is for all eternity the *self*-expression of God.[9]

In Jesus' Incarnation, human existence is found in its most basic and radical form. Therefore, the most important thing that we learn from Jesus is how to be fully human. What does it mean to be fully human? At the outset, we can note from the Incarnation that we are expressions of God; we are not *self*-expressions, and we are not God. We are not called to imitate Jesus as divine, but, rather, to imitate his *humanity*, and to fully accept our human existence as created in the image of God. To live as image of God is to be fully human; it is "the achievement in our turn of that assumption of human nature which the eternal Logos himself achieved."[10] Humanity as it exists in Jesus' actual life and destiny is the pattern of our lives. Everything about the life of Jesus embodies what is intended for us. He is our ultimate standard, a standard that can be measured by nothing other than Jesus himself and *his* life.

Jesus' Life

To believe in Jesus today is to accept the example of his life, and to listen to his message. To believe that Jesus is divine is to choose to make him our God. If we do not accept his life and message, then we choose to make someone or something else our god, and to devalue Jesus and what he stands for. Albert Nolan addresses this point when he says:

> Jesus himself changed the content of the word 'God.' If we do not allow him to change our image of God we will not be able to say that *he* is our Lord and our God. To choose him as our God is to make him the source of our information about divinity and to refuse to superimpose upon him our own ideas of divinity.[11]

The ultimate meaning of the Incarnation is that Jesus reveals God to us; God does not reveal Jesus to us. Knowing Jesus changes our understanding of the divine. To accept Jesus as our God is to accept "Abba" as our God; because of the hypostatic union, our God is both Jesus and Abba, yet they are distinct because it is Jesus alone who is visible to us.

The visible reality of Jesus is his life, death, and resurrection. Affirmations about Jesus are established in the four gospels; the letters of the apostles; non-Christian witnesses such as Flauvius, Josephus, Pliny the Younger, and the Talmud; and early Christianity. There is a "historical minimum" that we can claim about Jesus.[12] We know that he was a man. He was "chosen from among mortals" (Heb 5:1); born of a woman (Gal 4:4); and was a descendant of David (2 Tim 2:8). We also know that he shared our humanity: "Since, therefore, the children share flesh and blood, he himself likewise shared the same things..." (Heb 2:14).

Like all humans, Jesus lived in, and was part of, the religious milieu of his people and his historical situation. He was seen as a rabbi (Jn 1:38; 3:2; Mt 23:8), and in his capacity as such, he proclaimed divine law, taught in the synagogue, gathered disciples, and appealed to the authority of scripture. Unlike traditional rabbis, he also taught in open fields and on lakeshores. He was considered to be a prophet by those around him, a view that he declared of himself: "no prophet is accepted in the prophet's hometown" (Lk 4:24). He compared his own rejection to that of other prophets (Mt 23:37). This common opinion occurred to others: "It is a prophet, like one of the prophets of old" (Mk 6:15). It was the reaction of the crowds on his entry into Jerusalem: "This is the prophet Jesus from Nazareth in Galilee," (Mt 21:11), and their realization that "a great prophet has risen among us." (Lk 7:16) Prophets are called and sent and these qualities defined much of Jesus' lifestyle and message.

There is a notable difference in Jesus' message compared to that of other rabbis and prophets, however. Jesus speaks on his own authority: "You have heard that it was said to those of ancient times…. But I say to you…" (Mt 5:21-22). He uses "Amen" at the beginning of many of his statements indicating a special rapport with God. In a particular way, his claim to forgive sins highlights his authority (Mk 2:10; Mt 9:6; Lk 5:24), and in this means of reconciliation he is experienced as one who preaches and promises salvation. Above all, Jesus assumes a unique, personal relationship of intimacy with the God of Judaism. He addresses God as "Abba" (Mk 14:36). The intimate relationship that he has with God defines his whole way of being, and we see in Jesus a radically theocentric outlook on life. He proclaims God's kingdom; he has a filial relationship toward God as Father; he has a strong sense of obedience to God; and his prayer is a God-directed activity.

We also know from scripture that Jesus' lifestyle and message brought him into direct conflict with the religious and political leaders of his day, because, while he took part in the religious life of his people, he did intend to be a religious reformer. He broke the law, which had put itself in God's place, although this was not his real intention, and he fought against legalism in order to move beyond an ethic of pious sentiments. His death can never be isolated from the historical life that preceded it. In fact, it should be seen as the culminating point of his words and deeds. He set himself above the authority of Moses; he claimed to forgive sins; he initiated a reform of table fellowship; he promised salvation; and he criticized the established religious status quo.

The rejection of Jesus was inevitable for any Jew who was loyal to the law, since the authority of the law had become identified with the authority of God. The accusation of blasphemy was obvious: Jesus appeared to be assuming divine prerogatives and power. He must have reckoned with the possibility of death since he knew the destiny of other prophets. Jesus' decision to go to Jerusalem was the turning point in his life. It marked his departure from his Galilean ministry and his explicit refusal to accept the way of a political messiah. He accepted death as the inevitable consequence of fidelity to his mission to fulfill the will of God and to establish the kingdom of God on earth. It was his fidelity to the will of God that was the foundation of his radical preaching and his exhortations for reform, both of which were a call to conversion, and to gather disciples to follow him.

Jesus summons those who want to follow him to a radical conversion of life and faith. He is realistic about approaching people on moral grounds alone, and he breaks through ethical and religious formalism and establishes instead the reality of the deeply personal relationship that exists between humanity and a loving God. His preaching calls for repentance and conversion because he knows that God is ever-forgiving and ever-loving, and it is this forgiveness and love that is the constant pattern of his relationships with individuals.

Ironically, it was when people finally began to realize what Jesus was saying that his tragedy began. Most of his listeners were not ready for the total conversion, or the leap of faith, that his teaching demanded. Monika Hellwig points out that it was not that Jesus' message was misunderstood; rather, it was understood all too clearly:

> The kind of conversion to the coming and immanent Reign of God which he envisaged might look harmless enough in the beginning, but if it were really carried through it would cause a chain reaction that would shake human history from its very foundations, making a new earth in which the former pattern of privilege and power and wealth would make no sense at all.[13]

Jesus lived a life of love and this made him vulnerable. Few others were willing to place themselves in this kind of vulnerability. He lived as if it was God alone who decides human affairs, at all levels. This is not the way that most people live. Self-interest, ambition, and status dominate society now as then, and society is structured to sustain privilege. The basic pattern of human relationships is not a concern for the common good, or the reign of God, but for rampant self-interest.[14]

Jesus preached the common good by preaching to the poor and the oppressed and by giving them a sense of their own worth as created in the image of God. He offered them the promise of totally transforming their lives from living in fear and uncertainty to living in the ever-present love of God. For those who persecuted Jesus, his message presented much too great a threat to the established order. Jesus entered into the lives of those people who suffered the greatest injustices because this is where the compassion of God is most needed. Another powerful point made by Hellwig reminds us of this:

> Jesus crucified is a naked man among the stripped and unprotected of the world who cannot clothe themselves in the

privilege of power. And that is his last word to us. He died as he lived, among the poor and disregarded and unprivileged by his own choice. In death as in life he presents himself as simply human…simply a human being speaking out of his own vision of God, and the world and the meaning of life, to share that vision and the hope arising out of it with other human persons.[15]

Jesus left the world forever changed "by the haunting memory of his unrealized dream."[16] The message of God's love is still accessible to us. Jesus' good news of salvation is still available to all who want to respond, because in his resurrection the failure of Jesus is turned upside down. His resurrection from the dead is the triumph of God's word of hope and consolation to the world.

Jesus' Message

Jesus' message of hope and consolation to the world is that, although God is infinitely exalted, God loves each one of us. This is evident in the images of God that Jesus presents to us: a poor woman who scours her house to find one lost coin; a shepherd who watches over his sheep carefully, and who leaves the rest—his very livelihood—in order to search for one that is lost; and, perhaps the most powerful, a father who pines for his son because he is a part of his very self, and because the loss of his son is the loss of part of his own being (Lk 15:1-32).

Jesus does not simply present this love to us as a metaphor, however. He lives it by establishing a personal relationship with God, and by making the love of God a concrete reality, a part of human experience. He forgives and loves by taking up the cause of the "weak," eating with the "unclean," healing the sick, and socializing with the disadvantaged and with sinners. His witness is to his message of love, and in this witness he shows his disciples how they must live their lives. He summarizes how this can be done: "'You shall love the Lord your God with all your heart, and with all your soul, and with all your mind.' This is the greatest and first commandment. And a second is like it: 'You shall love your neighbour as yourself.' On these two commandments hang all the law and the prophets" (Mt 22:34-40). His message has two basic dimensions; it speaks of our attitude to our God and our attitude toward our neighbour. It is about right relationships: the relationship of the self to God, and of the self to neighbour. Jesus' total trust in God, and intimate relationship with God, allow him to know exactly how God wants these relationships to unfold. It is from the depths of this knowledge of love that his compassion for human suffering emanates. He has compassion for the poor and suffering because of their social hardships but, more importantly, because they are also alienated from the promise of the kingdom of God among them.

The right relationships between God, self, and neighbour are brought together in Jesus' teaching on the kingdom, which has God as its centre. The kingdom of God may be understood as the experience of right relationships between God and self, self and humanity, and humanity and all of creation. These relationships operate in a circular dynamic and not in a linear fashion; there is an ongoing interplay between all of these aspects, as seen in Jesus' exhortation on the kingdom. The way to establish the kingdom is to challenge prevailing injustices and to overcome traditional conflicts by reaching out to others in love and forgiveness, and to transcend the structures that perpetuate division. The kingdom is about justice and mercy, not revenge.

The heart of Jesus' message is God, and all of his teaching proclaims the immanence of God's reign. He presents his hearers with an absolute decision: for or against salvation, and salvation through God, which can only be lived in establishing God's reign. His proclamation was not about himself; he forgot himself for the sake of God, and for the salvation of his brothers and sisters. His message focused on the hope of the kingdom of God among us.

Jesus' teaching on the kingdom is summarized in the Beatitudes (Mt 5:1-11). The Beatitudes give us a description of what the kingdom of God looks like. It is a vision that turns our ideas upside down. Many people think that the Beatitudes are a paradox; they are, rather, a mirror that allows us to take a look at our lives, helps us to reflect our relationship with God, and permits us to adjust our lives, if necessary. If it is the poor who are blessed, then they are living kingdom lives; if the privileged are not blessed, then they must readjust themselves to reflect on the vision of the kingdom. The Beatitudes are a paradox in the realm of established world order, but not in the realm of truth and love. They touch us in the same way the rest of Jesus' teachings do. If we find them too difficult to accept, then we either want to adjust them, claim to misunderstand them, or in this case, say that they are really paradoxical. The message is clear if we can see it from the perspective of the love of God:

The beatitude we are promised confronts us with decisive moral choices. It invites us to purify our hearts of bad instincts and to seek the love of God above all else. It teaches us that true happiness is not found in riches or well-being, in human fame or power, or in any human achievement…but in God alone, the source of every good and of all love.[17]

The Beatitudes are part of the Sermon on the Mount (Mt 5–7), a discourse that Jesus spoke to his disciples in the early part of his ministry. Only those who fervently want to follow him are prepared to listen to, and to act upon, this challenging sermon. We know enough about Jesus to realize that he did nothing less than turn the world on its head.[18] He tells us that in the new order, the first shall be last and the outcast is the favourite, and he begins his beatitudes (or blessings) by stating that the poor are the blessed ones. This message was so impossible for people to comprehend that he eventually had to portray it with his own passion and death. His life, death, and resurrection turned human wisdom and judgment upside down. Paul calls this "the folly of the cross" (1 Cor 1:18-31). People did not understand, because the system that they were living in was essentially false. Why would he state that "the first will be last" if there was not something essentially wrong with the system in the first place?

So, what does Jesus tell us about this new order of the kingdom of God? First, the poor in spirit have the kingdom already. Being poor in spirit is crucial to all of Jesus' teaching and ministry. It means to be able to live without the need for your own reputation. It means that ego and personal ambition cannot be the motivations of your life. Anyone who is caught in personal ambition is trapped because they rely on the system for self-worth, but the more you are outside the system, the less you care about personal ambition, and the freer you are. Those who can live a poverty of spirit live their lives totally for God, and are, therefore, already living kingdom lives. Jesus states, "The kingdom of heaven *is* theirs"— not might be, or will be, but is right now.

He continues his discourse by promising that those who mourn now will be comforted. Weeping is a sign of compassion, and is drawn from the font of the love of God in our hearts. True compassion means that we weep with God for everyone, for both sides. Jesus also redefines the meaning of land. In his day, land was obtained and possessed by violence and oppression, but he builds on the teaching of the Hebrew scriptures that only God possesses the land. Poverty of spirit, compassion, and right use of land are followed by, and in a way brought together in, the next beatitude, which blesses the just.[19] Those who work for justice will be satisfied in abundance. To live a just life is to identify with the hungry, the poor, and those who weep, and is already a profound act of social justice. This blessing highlights the fact that the Beatitudes are not simply spiritual directives, but calls to social action.

Jesus pushes this call even further when he blesses the merciful. Mercy is beyond justice. Justice is what we deserve, but mercy is clemency, it is outside the realm of our predicaments. Justice is fairness in dealings with others, but mercy tempers justice with mildness and compassion. Mercy is undeserved; it is not owed to anyone. In this understanding of mercy in compassion and undeserved love, Jesus summarizes the whole gospel: to experience mercy is to experience the unconditional love of God, who reaches out to us. We cannot bargain with God for mercy or forgiveness. Our worth in God's eyes cannot be elevated by our achievements. Salvation is God's loving kindness that is forever. Mercy is the mystery of God's love, and in this love we see that mercy is relinquishing power over another. Rohr poignantly describes this relationship between mercy and power:

> The mystery of forgiveness is God's ultimate entry into powerlessness. Look at the times when you have withheld forgiveness. It's always your final attempt to hold a claim over the one you won't forgive. It's the way we finally hold on to power, to seek the moral high ground over another person.... [Nonforgiveness] is a form of power over another person, a way to manipulate, shame, control and diminish another. God in Jesus refuses all such power.[20]

Justice and mercy are the results of a pure heart, and Jesus continues his teaching by telling his disciples that it is the pure of heart who will see God. When we see with the heart, we see rightly.

Where justice, mercy, and right vision prevail, then there will be peace. The Beatitude for the peacemaker is the one and only time that the word "peacemaker" is used in the Bible. A peacemaker is the one who reconciles quarrels. Jesus is saying that there is no way to peace except by peacemaking itself. True and lasting peace can never be brought about by violence. Violence can stop conflict and war, but it cannot make peace. Those sent into a situation to maintain peace after a conflict are called peacekeepers, not peacemakers, because they keep peace by control and restraint, not by mercy and love. Theirs is an uneasy peace, not a lasting peace, and is often nothing more than a tense hiatus until the next conflict erupts.

One way of understanding this difference can be seen in Rohr's distinction between *Pax Romana* and *Pax Christi*. *Pax Romana* is the world's way of seeking control and calling it peace, but as Paul VI said, "There is no true peace without justice," and this is *Pax Christi*. Jesus connects his peace with justice and self-sacrifice: "*Pax Romana* creates a false peace by sacrificing others; the *Pax Christi* wants and works for true peace by sacrificing the false self of power, prestige and possessions."[21] We know that this will never become the national policy of any country, and Jesus knows that those who work for such kingdom peace will be persecuted. He knows that they will not be understood, and that the world will hate them. He also knows that "goodness can never be attacked directly; the messenger or the motivation have to be discredited."[22]

It is to all of these blessed ones that the kingdom of heaven belongs, and Jesus follows this part of his sermon by saying that those who live these Beatitudes are "the salt of the earth" and "the light of the world" (Mt 5:13-16). He challenges them by asking: If salt becomes tasteless, how can we salt the world with it? How can we be salt for the world if we do not believe and live the Gospel as Jesus has taught us? What hope do we have for offering an alternative to the destructive forces at work in our world today? By calling ourselves Christians, yet not following the way of our teachings, our message is bland and tasteless, and we do more harm than good. But to live as a light for the world is to live as Jesus taught us, as a shining truth that illuminates the darkness of injustice: "Let your light shine before others, so that they may see your good works and give glory to your Father in heaven" (Mt 5:16). Note that Jesus says *your* Father, and not *my* Father. He invites his disciples into the same relationship with God that he has.

Jesus' Beatitudes are not simply a set of prescriptions for getting to heaven. They are, rather, a set of descriptions of how to live a kingdom lifestyle in order to establish God's reign among us. They tell us how to live a life of discipleship, a life free of personal ambition and social power. When we live such poverty of spirit, when we weep, when we identify with the poor, when we work for justice and show mercy, when we make peace, and when we are joyful in the face of persecution, then we are his disciples. This is the power of God, although to many it seems to be powerlessness. The paradox is that when we act from this position of powerlessness, then the kingdom of God is among us.[23]

Jesus Teaches Us to Pray

When Jesus wants to summarize kingdom living for his disciples, he teaches through prayer. He connects prayer to kingdom living, and in so doing, he reminds us that our prayer is about active participation in the world around us; it is about establishing the kingdom here and now. Our prayer nourishes our kingdom activity, which is the culmination of our prayer. Prayer and discipleship are inseparable. It is not a coincidence, then, that Jesus' teaching on prayer follows closely after the Beatitudes in the discourse on discipleship. The Lord's Prayer (Mt 6:5-14), with an appended saying on forgiveness, is actually a synopsis of the whole discourse. It is a brief summary of the fundamentals of Jesus' teaching, and the heart of his message and mission: the kingdom of God.

Jesus not only taught the content of prayer of discipleship; his own actions witnessed to the need to pray. His life was saturated with prayer: "In the morning, while it was still very dark, he got up and went out to a deserted place, and there he prayed." (Mk 1:35); "after saying farewell to them, he went up on the mountain to pray" (Mk 6:46); "he went out to the mountain to pray; and he spent the night in prayer to God." (Lk 6:12). Particularly significant is that Jesus prays at critical moments in his ministry: before curing (Mk 9:29), when he preaches (Mt 11:25), and before his arrest in the garden of Gethsemane.

By including teachings on prayer in his discourse, Jesus marks prayer as one of the identifying characteristics of discipleship. William Thompson says that the disciples probably knew how to pray already, but to be a follower of Jesus was to pray in a different way.[24] In Luke's gospel, when the disciples asked, "Lord, teach us to pray," and when Jesus presents the Lord's Prayer in Matthew, this would not have been the first time that they were introduced to prayer. As Jews, they would probably recite the *Shema* in the morning and evening (Deut 6:4; 5-7), and pray the traditional blessing known as the *Tephilla* morning, afternoon, and evening. It is more likely that when the disciples asked Jesus to teach them to pray, they wanted to know what would be the particular characteristic form of prayer of his new disciples. Their request, "Lord, teach us to pray," in Luke is followed by "as John taught his disciples" (Lk 11:1).

Thompson also points out that Jesus' language for prayer is significant. The official liturgical language of the *Shema* and the *Tephilla* is Hebrew, but Jesus usually prays in Aramaic, which was the vernacular of the time:

> The address 'Abba' to the divine especially shows this, as well as the first two portions of the Our Father which echoes the *Kaddish,* the one prayer recited in the synagogue in Aramaic. In so doing, he removes prayer from the liturgical sphere of sacred language, and places it right in the midst of everyday life.[25]

In situating prayer in everyday life, Jesus is reiterating his conviction that the kingdom is also situated in everyday life. The Lord's Prayer is a prayer of hope and anticipation, of forgiveness and deliverance, but there is also some anticipation for these in present experience. In Jesus' teaching there is a tension between the kingdom that is near, and the kingdom that is yet to come. The prayer also shows his priorities. Our first concern must be for God's concerns, just as they were for Jesus, and then our needs will follow.[26] The prayer also expresses social needs. It is not just a prayer to God, but a petition for the arrival of the kingdom, for bread right now, and for the deliverance and protection from all that is evil. To pray as Jesus taught is not a private, individual communication with the divine, but a heightened awareness of, and sensitivity to, present injustices, and a concerted commitment to struggle against them.

Jesus' Ministry: Kingdom Living

Having shared with his disciples the requirements for being one of his followers, and having taught them how to pray, Jesus proceeded to witness to these in his kingdom-living. Jesus embodies his teaching through the example of his own life. He practises what he teaches: he embraces everyone with a purity of heart and with a humility grounded in the love of God. He is devoted to his mission, and even in the face of contradiction and threats, he remains obedient to his task to fulfill the will of God and to establish the kingdom among us. His ministry encourages his followers to take simple but radical steps toward others in trust, forgiveness, and loving solidarity. The impact of his presence on others was one of total acceptance, love, healing, and forgiveness in all aspects of their lives. Healing, whether physical or psychological, was always accompanied by spiritual renewal. Healing and forgiveness are the hallmarks of Jesus' ministry. Even his preaching, in and of itself, was redemptive because it anticipated the kingdom that he proclaimed.

Immediately in his ministry, Jesus acts against evil and suffering by driving out unclean spirits and by healing the sick. In Mark's gospel this is the beginning of a series of healings (Mk 1:21–2:12).

Jesus' ministry of forgiveness shows his direct contact with sinners and the marginalized. He went out of his way to socialize with tax collectors and prostitutes. He says of himself: "…the Son of Man came eating and drinking, and they say 'Look, a glutton and a drunkard, a friend of tax collectors and sinners!'" (Mt 11:19). He welcomed them and wanted to be their friend, and they responded because they knew that he had forgiven them. To forgive someone is to liberate them from past guilt, shame, and fear, and the hold that these feelings have over them. God forgives by overlooking our past and taking away any consequences of past transgressions.[27] This is precisely what Jesus did. He overlooked people's past and refused to hold anything against them. He treated them as people who did not deserve rejection; they were forgiven. They were loved and they knew it, which is why grateful love and uncontrollable joy were often people's reactions to encounters with Jesus. Their jubilant reaction was a sign of the liberation that they felt when they were healed and forgiven. The entirety of Jesus' ministerial activity was totally directed to disrupting the context of evil and, thus, opening the way for such new attitudes, behaviours, and relationships.

The people who encountered Jesus in this way were not passive recipients of dispensed forgiveness. In these encounters, Jesus deliberately points to the power of their own faith. For example, he says to the woman who washed his feet, "Your sins are forgiven.…Your faith has saved you; go in peace" (Lk 7:48, 50). This is an astonishing claim. Jesus, as a Jew, would believe that "for God all things are possible" (Mk 10:27), but he differs by saying that everything is possible for *anyone who has faith:* "All things can be done for one who believes (Mk 9:23).… if you have faith the size of a mustard seed, you will say to this mountain, 'Move from here to there,' and it will move; and nothing will be impossible for you" (Mt 17:20). Faith, in this context, is a personal conviction. It is not simply assent to a doctrine about God, but the conviction that God is good and will triumph over evil.[28] Faith for the sick person is that they can and will be cured. This is their faith in the power of God at work in their lives. Jesus' ministry shows the power of God at work in the world liberating people because of the faith that Jesus motivated in them. Just to be in the company of Jesus was a liberating experience, and it made people feel safe and secure. To be with Jesus was to be in the kingdom of God and, as Nolan points out:

> It was not necessary to fear evil spirits, evil men or women or storms on the lake. They did not have to worry about how they would be clothed or what they would eat, or about falling sick. It was remarkable how frequently Jesus is said to have reassured and encouraged them with words like: 'Don't be afraid;' 'Don't worry,' or 'Cheer up.' (Mk 5:36; 6:50; Mt 6:25, 27, 28, 31, 34; 9:2, 22; 10:19, 26, 28, 31; 14:27; Lk 12:32; Jn 16:33)....Jesus not only healed and forgave them, he also dispelled their fears and relieved them of their worries. His very presence liberated them.[29]

II. Loving Discipleship/Public Ministry

Fundamental to Jesus' ministry of liberation is his sense of being sent by God. In turn, he sends out his disciples to continue and extend his message and his ministry. When he sends them out he makes one thing clear:

> "...you are not to be called rabbi, for you have one teacher, and you are all students. And call no one your father on earth, for you have one Father—the one in heaven. Nor are you to be called instructors, for you have one instructor, the Messiah." (Mt 23:8-10)

We often talk about Jesus' ministry as public, because the very nature of ministry includes its public aspect. One can never talk about "private" ministry; all ministry is for, and in relationship with, others. Ministry is a public service performed on behalf of the Christian community for the promotion of the kingdom of God as Jesus portrays it. The foundation of this ministry is discipleship. Discipleship was what was meant for his first followers to be in relationship to the pre-Easter Jesus; it is also what it means to followers in every generation to be in relationship to the post-Easter Jesus. The story and meaning of discipleship are not just about people in the past; they are also about us. Discipleship calls us to be like Jesus. The more we imitate Jesus, the more we are formed into his likeness. Following Jesus in discipleship transforms us into more compassionate human beings. Thus, it would not be facetious to suggest that we go back and reread what has been said about Jesus' life, message, and ministry in this chapter, because these are the foundations for our ministry today. That being said, let us consider some of the major developments in our understanding of discipleship.

Since discipleship in the New Testament is following after, or journeying with, Jesus, an understanding of discipleship is therefore not limited to the Twelve Apostles. In the New Testament, we see the terms "the Twelve," the "Apostles," and the "disciples." Not all of the disciples were apostles, and not all of the apostles were members of the Twelve, but all of the Twelve were apostles, and all of the apostles were disciples. This distinction is important. Discipleship is not limited to official members of the community.

"Apostle" is from the Greek word *apostolis,* meaning "one who is sent." It was a function or office within early Christianity. The New Testament writers refer to various individuals and groups in the early church as apostles, but the meaning of the term and the extent of its application are matters of dispute. In spite of the theory of apostolic succession that developed as part of the church's doctrine of ministry, the title and office of "apostle" were not transferable; the title died with its original bearers. For Luke, an apostle had to be someone who had accompanied Jesus from his baptism until his ascension, and who could be a witness to the resurrection (Acts 1:15-26). In the second century, the apostles were understood as part of the inspired foundational stage of Christianity, but were not seen as a contemporary reality.[30] The church has never had apostles in the New Testament sense since the first century.[31] When applied to individuals in later Christian literature, the use of the term is metaphorical. There was a tendency very early in the post-apostolic age to limit the title to the Twelve, plus Paul, James, and Barnabas, and certain members of the second generation continued to use the title. This is evident from scripture: "I know your works, your toil and your patient endurance. I know that you cannot tolerate evildoers; you have tested those who claim to be apostles but are not, and have found them to be false" (Rev 2:2). Here, the term is used against those who were not teaching the Gospel of Jesus, and whose claim was attacked by orthodox leaders as fraudulent. The rise of heresy impelled the early church community to limit the final authority for its doctrine and practice to the teaching and example of the founder-apostles. Thus, by the middle of the second century we have an "Apostles' Creed," a New Testament canon of writings ascribed to the apostles or to their immediate disciples, and a hierarchical ministry that claims succession from the apostles.[32] Those true to the apostolic succession were those ministers who vowed to teach the gospel of Jesus Christ and to witness to his teaching in an exemplary way. Early Christian communities claimed validity for their ministry on the basis of the apostolic succession of the community leaders.

Ultimately, whether one is a member of the Twelve, an apostle, or a community leader bound by the gospel, one is first and foremost called to be a disciple. The picture of discipleship which the New Testament authors present is meant for *all* followers of Jesus, not just a chosen few. A disciple is one who shares the life of, and imitates, a master. Disciple is the name most frequently given to those around Jesus who accept him as master (Mt 5:1; Lk 6:17; 19:37). People who travel with Jesus (Lk 8:1-3) or listen to his teaching in faith (Lk 10:23) are disciples.

Being a disciple of Jesus means journeying with him from the life of conventional wisdom to the alternative wisdom of life in the Spirit. Discipleship can only be understood by someone who takes the risk to love Jesus personally. As Rahner says: "…every encounter with the concrete man Jesus is an ever unique discipleship."[33] To journey with him is to believe in him. To believe in him is to love God with our whole mind, heart, and soul, and to reach out and be this same love for our neighbour, that is, everyone we encounter. Love for one's neighbour is the actualization of discipleship, but as Borg reminds us, this is not always easy, and many times we flounder: "To journey with Jesus means listening to his teaching—sometimes understanding it, sometimes not quite getting it. It can involve denying him, even betraying him."[34] Being a disciple also means living in community, becoming part of the alternative community of Jesus: a community of compassion that remembers and celebrates who Jesus is, and what he has done for us. Discipleship is not an individual path. Disciples always journey with a company of other disciples. Jesus' disciples always had a companion, someone with whom to share bread, and their mission was to form a community of similar followers.

New Testament discipleship is the guiding norm for ministry and community in the church today. Questions of ministry in any faith community will never be satisfactorily resolved unless we go back to our understanding of Jesus himself. What we do in ministry will ultimately be conditioned by what we believe about Jesus. It will also, however, be conditioned by what we believe about the human person. Christology and theological anthropology are intimately related, and this is nowhere clearer than in the hypostatic union: when God became human in the person of Jesus Christ, God opened up the potential for every human person to participate in the infinite mystery of the divine. When we open ourselves to a life of discipleship in imitation of the humanity of Jesus, we fully accept our existence as created in the image of God. The awesome reality of the hypostatic union is that, created as expressions of God, we really are, in our humanity, able to participate in the infinite mystery of God. What tremendous strength and passion we can bring to our ministry when we fully appropriate this action of God for us in Jesus Christ.

There is always, then, a mutual relationship between ministry in the faith community and our christology; the bridge between these two is discipleship. Discipleship is *the* foundation for an understanding of shared ministry. It can also illuminate a discussion in contemporary Catholic theology, which Kenan Osborne articulates as follows:

> What is the difference between the priesthood of all believers and the ordained or ministerial priesthood? The attempts to describe or define either of these two 'priesthoods' by comparing and contrasting them one with the other seems to lead nowhere. Rather, it seems to me, one should search out the very meaning of both priesthoods, and this theological foundation or base is that of discipleship.[35]

Thus, when we want to understand the meaning and role of such terms as People of God, priesthood of all believers, ministerial priesthood, religious life, and the cleric/lay structure, then we must look to Christian discipleship. The New Testament description of discipleship is the basis from which to describe all of these categories, "and it is the grid against which they are judged for Christian validity."[36]

Ultimately, Jesus is the model, not only for Christian leadership, but for every Christian; there is no double standard of discipleship. Belief and conversion are fundamental aspects of discipleship, and this conversion is open to all without exception. There are not two ways of discipleship, one for those who hold a leadership role in the church and one for everyone else in the church. *All* who believe in Jesus must strive for discipleship in their lives. Whether or not one is a leader in the community, one must reflect the same image of discipleship.

Discipleship is not easy, but if we are sincere in our desire to serve in God's kingdom, then we will not have to do it alone, and Jesus has assured us of this. While he was still with them, Jesus made a promise to his disciples:

> "I will ask the Father, and he will give you another Advocate, to be with you forever. This is the Spirit of truth, whom the world cannot receive, because it neither sees him nor knows him. You know him because he abides with you, and he will be in you." (Jn 14:16-17)

This Advocate that the Father sends to be with us is the Holy Spirit, the third Person of the Trinity. A discussion of the Holy Spirit within the context of the Trinity will complete our understanding of the Christian God in revelation, and will lay a deeper foundation for who we are in relation to our God, and how we are called to minister.

Chapter 4

Trinity: God-Within-Us

[Jesus] came and proclaimed peace to you who were far off and peace to those who were near; for through him both of us have access in one Spirit to the Father. So then you are no longer strangers and aliens, but you are citizens with the saints and also members of the household of God, built upon the foundations of the apostles and prophets, with Christ Jesus himself as the cornerstone. In him the whole structure is joined together and grows into a holy temple in the Lord; in whom you also are built together spiritually into a dwelling place for God. (Eph 2:17-22)

Introduction

The doctrine of the Trinity is the Christian understanding of God. We have already begun our exposition of the Trinity by discussing God the Father in Chapter 2, and God the Son in Chapter 3. In the description of the mission and ministry of Jesus, we saw the work of the Trinity in the world. In fulfilling the will of the Father, Jesus accomplishes the salvific dimension of his relationship within the Trinity. To complete our understanding of God, we must include a discussion of the Holy Spirit, the third Person of the Trinity. A theology of the Trinity will further our appreciation of Jesus' mission, and will deepen our resolve to continue this mission in our ministry, especially the call to live as a Spirit-filled faith community inspired by the indwelling of the Spirit.

Discussions in trinitarian theology are usually structured around the distinction between the "immanent" Trinity and the "economic" Trinity. These terms are widely accepted in both Catholic and Protestant theology.

They were first introduced by Rahner, and are considered to be the most helpful way to understand what can often seem a very difficult, even incomprehensible, doctrine. The immanent Trinity is the reality of the three divine Persons as they exist together in mutual relationship. The economic Trinity is the reality of the three divine Persons as they are for us in revelation. In the economic reality of the Trinity, we witness the distinct salvific dimension of each of the divine Persons: God is the creator, Jesus is the redeemer, and the Holy Spirit is the sanctifier. In these dimensions, each Person of the Trinity is both a means and an example of what it is to create, redeem, and sanctify. They are fulfilled in creation, in which God brings us into being, they are incarnated in Jesus' response to the will of the Father, and they are evident in the sanctifying and sustaining work of the Holy Spirit.

We see from the work of the economic Trinity that the three divine Persons subsist in an intimate relationship with one another. The Father does not act alone, Jesus does not act alone, nor does the Holy Spirit. Our God is a triune God, a God of loving, trinitarian communion. A community of loving relationships is *the* identifiable characteristic of the Trinity. This characteristic calls us to live a life of similar loving relationships, and defines our ministry. The very nature of the economic Trinity calls us into a life of unity and loving communion.

We are given the Holy Spirit so that the Spirit can live in us, and so that we can continue Jesus' kingdom work. At Pentecost, the Spirit came upon those who said "yes" to a new life in the Spirit, and who made the promise to continue Jesus' mission. The Spirit is also alive in those who make this same declaration of mission today. When we minister, we are being Spirit for the world. All Christian ministry is a sign of the work of the Holy Spirit. Everyone involved in ministry is called to internalize the truth that the divine presence that Jesus brought into the world goes on forever in all people, through the power of the Holy Spirit. The Spirit cannot function in the world, however, without our faithful response to our call to discipleship. The Spirit dwells within us as an embodied reality. Often we do not admit this, much less accept the active responsibility that it requires, because it means that God needs us to be love and service in the world: to be Spirit alive!

I. The Mystery of the Triune God

The doctrine of the Trinity summarizes the central truth of Christianity: we are saved by God, through Jesus Christ, by the power of the Holy Spirit. Yet the Trinity is also one of the most incomprehensible of Christian teachings. It is a mystery in the strictest sense of the word. A mystery is something about which we would know nothing were it not for God revealing it to us, and which is not wholly intelligible even after such revelation. What can such an incomprehensible teaching possibly tell us about everyday Christian living and ministry? It is important to keep in mind that the positive element of any mystery is that the grace of our loving God helps us to understand its truth. Rahner urges:

> We should never forget that our theology is not just the product of human cleverness.... Even when we are speaking about the mystery of the life of the triune God we are not speaking in mere concepts, but from experience, because prior to all theology, the Spirit, who searches the deep things of God, has already become our Spirit.[1]

In other words, our understanding of God-in-Christ occurs only because we have been drawn by the Holy Spirit who dwells within us. The drawing of the Spirit within us is the activity of faith. Once again we see the transcendental nature of the human person at work: the doctrine of the Trinity presupposes belief in God together with God's activity in Jesus, and this presupposes an awareness of the transcendent Other as the one who generates this awareness. This, in turn, presupposes the awareness of ourselves as transcendent beings. Thus, the doctrine of the Trinity presupposes a theology of revelation, a theology of Christ, and a theological anthropology. It summarizes what we have been doing up to this point, and sets the agenda for our theology of church, and for sacramental theology. It will also solidify the foundation for our theological anthropology.

God's Nature and the Activity of God in the World

When we talk about the threefold quality that distinguishes God's nature, we are referring to the immanent Trinity. Immanence in the Trinity is the reciprocal relationships of the Father, the Son, and the Holy Spirit *to each other*. When we talk about the economic Trinity, we are referring to the three manifestations of God's activity in the world, corresponding to the names Father, Son, and Holy Spirit. It also denotes the "missions" of the Trinity: the sending and communication of the Father, the Son, and the Holy Spirit in their work of redemption and sanctification. These missions establish communion between the triune God and humanity. The economic Trinity is described in the scriptural accounts of God's self-revelation where we have Jesus, the Son, the Father to whom he prayed, and the Holy Spirit at work in the minds and hearts of individual believers and in the world.

The distinction between the immanent and the economic Trinity is strictly conceptual. There are not two trinities. There is one God, one divine self-communication, manifest in creation, redemption, and sanctification. The immanent and the economic Trinity are identical. Unless the two missions and the two Persons in whom God comes to us are part of God's very self, we cannot speak of a *self*-communication of God. If the way in which we know God does not disclose the triune way in which God really is, then God has not revealed God's own self, and there is another God who remains hidden behind the God who is revealed.[2] This would mean that who God is for us tells us absolutely nothing about who God is in God's own self: triune. Our scriptures, however, conclude otherwise. The immanent Trinity is known to us in faith because we have seen the economic Trinity at work in the history of our salvation.

We did not first hear about the immanent Trinity and then look to see how it becomes a reality in our lives. Rather, our understanding of the immanent Trinity comes out of our experience of the practical saving activities of the triune God as we witness them. Therefore, the doctrine of the Trinity is not a speculative doctrine alone. It is the way we express our fundamental relationship with God, and God's relationship with us. The economic Trinity is not the means of gaining knowledge of the immanent Trinity, but it is the same thing. Participation in the triune reality of God in history also means participation in the eternal relationality of God. The economic Trinity is the immanent Trinity and vice versa, and, as we saw in the hypostatic union, it allows for a correlation between God's self-communication in history, and God's eternal triune being. Alister McGrath provides the following helpful summary of the economic and immanent Trinity:

> The God who is known in the economy of salvation corresponds to the way in which God actually is. They are the same God.

God's self-communication takes on a threefold form because God is *in se* threefold. God's self-revelation corresponds to God's essential nature.

Human experience of God's activity in the economy of salvation is also experience of God's inner history and immanent life. There is only one network of divine relationships; that network exists in two distinct forms, one eternal, and the other historical. One is above history, the other is shaped and conditioned by the limiting factors of history.[3]

The Trinity Revealed in Scripture

The doctrine of the Trinity cannot be found in either the Old Testament or the New Testament. There are, however, some essential elements of what eventually became the doctrine in these writings. In the Old Testament, the Trinity looms in outline as a mystery waiting to be disclosed. McBrien explains:

> The Old Testament is pre-Christian and as such does not provide any trinitarian understanding of God. This is not to say that the Old Testament's understanding of God is utterly inconsistent with the subsequent trinitarian development of the Christian era.... While it would be theologically unjustifiable to suggest some 'foreshadowing' of the Trinity in the Old Testament, the personification of certain divine forces (the 'Word,' the 'Wisdom,' the 'Spirit' of God) which are distinct from God and the world provides a certain prelude to the Christian understanding of God as triune.[4]

In the Word of God, God's speech is treated as an entity independent of God, yet which has its origins in God. The Word is portrayed as going forth into the world to comfort people, and to bring them guidance, judgment, and salvation (Ps 119:89; Ps 147:15-20; Isa 55:10-11). The personification of God as Wisdom is especially evident in the Wisdom literature—Proverbs, Job, and Sirach—which treats the attribute of divine wisdom as if it were a person, with an existence that is apart from, yet dependent upon, God. Wisdom, which is always personified as female, fashions the world in an ongoing actuality of creation (Prov 1:20-23; 9:1-6; Job 28; Sir 24). In the Old Testament, the "Spirit" of God refers to

God's presence and power within creation. The Spirit is also portrayed as being present in the expected messiah (Isa 42:1-3), and as being the agent of a new creation that will surpass the old order (Ezek 36:26; 37:1-14). From these personifications, we can see that a unitarian conception of God proved inadequate to contain this dynamic understanding of God. This pattern of divine activity is expressed in the doctrine of the Trinity.[5]

While the revelation of the Trinity is found in the New Testament, this collection of writings does not contain any well-established doctrine. Doctrine involves questioning, reflection, and the systematization of ideas. Doctrine about the Trinity did not arise until almost two centuries later, when Christians began to articulate their experience of the divinity of Jesus and the Holy Spirit. This is most evident in the writings of Tertullian, the Latin Christian and apologist from Roman Africa (ca. 160–ca. 225). While most scripture scholars and theologians agree that the New Testament does not set out an explicit doctrine of the Trinity, they also maintain that the trinitarian doctrine has its origins in the testimony of this scripture.

The New Testament witnesses to the divinity of Jesus, the Son. The Son is understood to be in the realm of the divine when he is referred to as pre-existent (Jn 1:1; Phil 2:6-11). He is the presence of the reign of God (Mt 12:28; Lk 11:20), he has lordship over the sabbath (Mk 2:23-28; 3:1-6), and he possesses the fullness of the Spirit (Lk 4:18). The New Testament writers were also aware of the divinity of the Holy Spirit. Yet, as the presence of God, the Son and the Spirit are not seen as simply the One whom they reveal; they are distinguished from God in some way, and each has a particular and distinct relationship to God. Thus, while the New Testament firmly adheres to the uniqueness of God, it also recognizes a triplicity: Father, Son, and Holy Spirit, who are distinguished from one another by their different salvific functions, and yet who are so equal among themselves that the Son and the Spirit cannot be thought of as mere forces of God's work in the world. The New Testament does not, however, specify the terms of the relationships between the Father and the Son, nor among the Father, Son, and Holy Spirit. It assumes only that there is some relationship: the Father sends the Son and the Holy Spirit (Jn 14:16, 26; 17:3; Gal 4:6), and gives the Spirit through the Son (Jn 15:26; 16:7). The very assumption of these relationships is significant, however.

A distinction between the three Persons follows from the fact that the words Father, Son, and Holy Spirit are not used interchangeably, but beside one another in the same context. This is particularly evident in the so-called "threefold formulas," that is, in the ways of speaking in which Father, Son, and Holy Spirit always appear together. The most significant, and probably the best known of these formulas, is in Matthew's gospel: "Go therefore and make disciples of all nations, baptizing them in the name of the Father and of the Son and of the Holy Spirit" (Mt 28:19). In Christian baptism, believers are introduced to, and initiated into, the community of the Trinity, and are under its protection.

A second significant trinitarian text in the New Testament is found in the writings of Paul. This text is now used in all celebrations of the Eucharist: "The grace of the Lord Jesus Christ, the love of God, and the communion of the Holy Spirit be with all of you" (2 Cor 13:13). Paul's writings highlight the community of the Trinity, which acts on our behalf: "But it is God who establishes us with you in Christ and has anointed us, by putting his seal on us and giving us his Spirit in our hearts as a first installment" (2 Cor 1:21-22). "For through him [Jesus] both of us have access in one Spirit to the Father" (Eph 2:18).

Such references to the coming of salvation imply an immanent Trinity, and any understanding of the Trinity that is evident in the New Testament is oriented toward the economy of salvation. God and the Father are synonyms, and the Son and the Spirit are spoken of inasmuch as they come into the experience of faith as the actual presence of God in the history of salvation. Thus, although the modern conception of personality is not distinguished in the three, the New Testament does make the distinctions affirmed in the doctrine of the Trinity. The language of the New Testament makes it clear that Jesus is for us the very being of God among us, and yet he is not the Father. The Spirit is experienced as the self-giving of God, but in such a way that the Spirit allows us to experience the illimitability of the God the Father.

The doctrine of the Trinity is the outcome of a process of critical reflection by the first Christians on the patterns of this divine activity revealed in scripture and continued in Christian experience.

Early Historical Development of the Trinity

Early Christians gradually came to certain conclusions about the inner reality of God based on their own experience of God's activity in the world. They began to wonder whether there was more to God than traditional monotheism suggests. They speculated on whether there were three gods, or perhaps a small community of unequal gods. In light of Jesus' deeds and the manifestations of the Holy Spirit, Christians drew the conclusion that God the Father had sent the Son and the Holy Spirit, and that the three together are God in communion. As the early church progressively reflected on its experience of God, it concluded that the God whom we experience as triune in history—the economic Trinity—must also have a triune nature. That is, the inner life of the Godhead—the immanent Trinity—must also be triune.

In the beginning, the Trinity was articulated in prayer and worship rather than in theological statements. In doxologies—prayers of praise and thanksgiving—the faithful gave witness to the presence of the Father, the Son, and the Holy Spirit, and all of their prayers ended, then as now, with "Glory be to the Father, through the Son, in the unity of the Holy Spirit."

Trinitarian faith was evident in sacramental practice. In keeping with the command of Jesus, Christians were baptized in the name of the Father, and of the Son, and of the Holy Spirit. The first eucharistic formulas were also trinitarian in their structure. The Father is always the end and objective of every celebration, the Son's Paschal mystery is celebrated, and the Spirit's activity in the community is recalled. Everything that is done in the Eucharist is done in praise and worship to bring the faithful into trinitarian communion. A clear trinitarian awareness is also evident in the statements of the Christian creed: "I believe in God, the Father almighty…and in Jesus Christ, his only Son, our Lord…. I believe in the Holy Spirit." Finally, even today, we are accustomed to making the sign of the cross, which is an expression of faith in the triune God. These experiences of prayer, sacrament, and liturgy began the early church's theological reflection on what they were doing and celebrating.

The main theological question facing the church in the immediate post-biblical period was the relationship of Jesus, the Son, to God. At this time, the Spirit was regarded as a synonym for God, but that could not be true of the Son, since he had specific roles, and was perceived as having an identity that was distinct from the Father. As we have seen in our section on christology, Jesus' co-equal divinity was of the highest urgency, not because of doctrinal consistency, but because our salvation was at stake. A consensus emerged that Jesus was not of a *similar* substance as God (Greek: *homoiousios*), but rather of the *same* substance (Greek: *homoousios*). If Jesus was God in any meaningful sense, what did this imply about God? Were there now two gods? The more emphatic the church became that Jesus was God, the more it came under pressure to clarify how Jesus related to God. One of the biggest difficulties was finding language with which to articulate this divine mystery. References to three Persons and one substance may be confusing, but understanding how the terms came to emerge can be helpful.

Tertullian is attributed with the development of the distinctive trinitarian terminology. His teaching marks the passage from a cosmological understanding of the Trinity to a consideration of its inner life through the missions of the Word and the Spirit. Tertullian's language for the doctrine of the Trinity is still valuable today.

Some scholars question Tertullian's use of the word "substance." They debate whether this term makes the Father and the Son equal, or makes the Son subordinate to the Father. For some, "substance" seems too limited, too much like the material substance of earthly reality. Most, however, accept Tertullian's description of God's oneness as "substance," and each of the three as "persons." He created the rational language of the trinitarian faith.

Tertullian introduced the Latin term *persona* (person) to translate the Greek word *hypostasis,* which had been gaining acceptance in the Greek-speaking church. Scholars have debated at length what he meant by this Latin term.[6] McGrath's explanation casts some light on the complexities of trinitarian doctrine:

> The term *persona* literally means a 'mask' such as that worn by an actor in a Roman drama. At this time actors wore masks to allow the audience to understand which of the different characters in the drama they were playing. The term *persona* then came to have a developed meaning along the lines of 'the role that someone is playing.' It is quite possible that Tertullian wanted his readers to understand the idea of 'one substance, three persons' to mean that the one God played three distinct, yet related roles in the great drama of human redemption. Behind the plurality of roles lay a single actor. The complexity of this process of creation and redemption did not imply that there were many

gods, simply that there was one God who acted in a multiplicity of manners within 'the economy of salvation.'[7]

"Person" distinguishes the Father, Son, and Holy Spirit individually within the unity of God. Each Person is in full relationship with the others, and surrenders to the others so that the Father is fully in the Son, and in the Holy Spirit, and so on for each Person in turn.

Tertullian introduced the term "substance'" to express the idea of a fundamental unity within the Godhead, despite the Persons' outward appearance of diversity. Substance is what the three Persons in the Trinity have in common, and does not exist independent of the three Persons. Substance expresses one sole divine nature. It is what unites the Trinity and makes the three Persons one God.

Perichoresis: *How the Persons of the Trinity Relate to One Another*

The fundamental unity of the Trinity is its most significant characteristic. Whenever we speak of the Trinity, we must think of the communion of the Father, the Son, and the Holy Spirit. To explain the interdependence of the three divine Persons, Orthodox theologians coined a term that began to spread in the seventh century, especially as used by St. John Damascus (d. 750): *perichoresis*.

Perichoresis (Latin: *circumincession*; English: reciprocal interpenetration) refers to the way the Persons of the Trinity are in relation to one another. Each person maintains a distinctive identity while sharing in the life of the others, who also share in that Person's life, in turn. *Perichoresis* emphasizes that there is a mutual and reciprocal communion of being in the Trinity that expresses the love and the life that constitute the nature of God.

The result of this mutual and reciprocal communion is community. To say that God is communion means that the three Persons are turned toward one another. In the immanence of the Trinity there exists not the solitude of One, but the communion of three unique ones. A further development of the term "person" can help with this understanding of communion. While "person" may be understood as individuality, existing in and of itself, distinct from any other, in terms of relationship and reciprocity, a person is a being who is always open to others. "Person" is a being-in-relationship. No person can be thought of by himself or herself apart from other persons. Leonardo Boff provides some further insights into this aspect of *perichoresis* through the use of an analogy:

In each human existence we discover the following relationships: there is always an I–Thou relation. The I is never alone; it echoes a Thou reverberating with the I. The Thou is another I, different and open to the I of the other. It is in this play of I–Thou dialogue that the human person gradually builds his or her personality.

But the I–Thou dialogue is not all there is. There is also the communion between the I-and-Thou. Communion arises when I and Thou are expressed together, when they overcome the I and Thou and together from a new relationship, the WE. To say WE is to reveal community.[8]

Boff believes that something similar to this takes place in the Trinity. The Father and the Son are united and reveal the WE—it is the Holy Spirit. The divine communion results from the relationships among the three divine Persons. Their communion is so deep, and so radical, that they are a single God. We cannot speak of one Person without speaking of the other two as well. Everything that is said of the Father is said also of the Son, and everything that is said of the Son and the Father is said also of the Holy Spirit, and so on in their common unity.

Another effect of this reciprocal interpenetration is that each Person dwells in the other: this is a second meaning of *perichoresis*. Boff explains:

In simple words it means that the Father is ever in the Son, communicating life and love to him. The Son is ever in the Father knowing him and lovingly acknowledging him as life and love. The Holy Spirit is in the Son and the Father as source and manifestation of life and love of this boundless source. The Council of Florence defined it well in 1441:'The Father is wholly in the Son and wholly in the Holy Spirit; the Son is wholly in the Father and wholly in the Holy Spirit; the Holy Spirit is wholly in the Father and wholly in the Son. None precedes the other in eternity, none exceeds the other in greatness, or excels the other in power.'[9]

The Trinity is a mystery of absolute inclusivity. Such intimacy prevents us from understanding one Person without the others. The three Persons do not exist first singly and then relate to one another; in their immanence, they are interconnected, and live together eternally.

Where Does the Holy Spirit Come From? The Filioque *Debate*

Part of the debate concerning the distinctiveness of the three divine Persons and their unity gave rise to a conflict on the procession of the Holy Spirit. In the Trinity, a procession means a coming forth from another; it relates to the way, and order, in which one Person proceeds from another. There are two processions: the generation of the Son, and the spiration of the Holy Spirit. In John's gospel, Jesus sends the Spirit from the Father, and the Spirit proceeds from the Father: "When the Advocate comes, whom I will send to you from the Father, the Spirit of truth who comes from the Father, he will testify on my behalf" (Jn 15:26). There has been a great deal of theological debate regarding the interpretation of this procession. The question is, does the Holy Spirit proceed from the Father alone or from the Father *and* the Son? This issue, known as the *filioque* (Latin: "and from the Son") controversy, is still a point of conflict between Roman Catholic (Latin theology) and Orthodox (Greek theology) churches.[10]

In Latin theology, there are two processions: 1) The Son proceeds from the Father, and 2) the Holy Spirit proceeds from the Father *and* the Son. In Greek theology, there are also two processions: 1) The Son proceeds from the Father, and 2) the Holy Spirit proceeds from the Father *through* the Son. While the churches differ in their understanding of the procession of the Holy Spirit, both churches agree that God the Father does not proceed, since the Father is unbegotten and unoriginated. The Father comes from no one.

Greek theology begins with the Father as the source of divinity. The Father sends the Son, and the Holy Spirit emerges simultaneously. Latin theology begins with the single divine nature (substance), which is the same in each of the Persons. In generating the Son, the Father entrusts everything to him, including the ability to join with the Father in spirating the Holy Spirit: "All that the Father has is mine" (Jn 16:15). Greek theologians reject this interpretation because they believe that it sacrifices the specific feature of the Father, that of being the single source of all divinity. If the Son shares this single source of divinity, then it would cease to be single and he would be a kind of second Father. Both theologies assure the full divinity and equality of the Son and the Holy Spirit, but their approach is different. Greek theology understands the Son and the Holy Spirit proceeding from the same source: the Father. Latin theology takes another route, insisting that the three divine Persons are "consubstantial": together in the same substance. The Holy Spirit has the same nature that the Son received from the Father, which is why they conclude that the Holy Spirit proceeds from the Father *and* the Son.

To affirm the belief that the Holy Spirit proceeds from both the Father and the Son, the Roman church, the church in the West, added the phrase *filioque* to the Nicene creed in the sixth century: *Credo…in Spiritum Sanctum…qui ex Patre Filioque procedit* (We believe…in the Holy Spirit…who proceeds from the Father and the Son). To affirm the *filioque* is to affirm that the Spirit is not given to us independently of the Son. The first official proclamation of a creed with the addition of the *filioque* is found in the documents of the third council of Toledo (589). However, in 810, Pope Leo III, while he agreed theologically with the clause, rejected its use in the liturgy. This was not rescinded until 1024, when Pope Benedict VIII gave his approval. In this revised creed, the Holy Spirit is said to proceed from the Father *and* the Son. The Greek church, the church in the East, rejected the *filioque*, and affirmed that the Spirit proceeds *only* from the Father. Western theologians maintain that the *filioque* doctrine declares that Jesus and the Spirit are inseparable, which emphasizes the unity of God. For Eastern theologians, however, the *filioque* subordinates the Spirit to Jesus, and thus promotes a Spirit-deficient christology and an understanding of church in which power is divorced from spiritual presence.

That God is triune, as opposed to *how* God is triune, is the clear and consistent official magisterium or teaching of the church. The important elements of this teaching can be summarized as follows:

- One God exists in three Persons, and each of these Persons is one divine nature (substance); therefore they are each equally eternal and almighty.
- The Three Persons are distinct from one another: the Father is the original possession of the divinity; the Son is begotten by the Father; and the Holy Spirit proceeds from the Father and the Son.
- Through these distinctions of Father, Son, and Holy Spirit, there are relations and properties in God that are distinct from God's nature.
- Each divine Person is wholly in each of the others (*perichoresis*), each in the one triune God.

How Are We Related to the Holy Spirit?

We have already seen how our relationship to God is through our creation in God's image, and our relationship to Jesus in the hypostatic union. Both of these are fundamental principles of theological anthropology. If we are so intimately related to God the Father and to Jesus the Son then, according to trinitarian doctrine, we must be similarly related to the Holy Spirit. The revelation of the Holy Spirit, especially in the New Testament, shows something about how we are related to the Spirit.

The revelation of the Holy Spirit in the New Testament takes place in privileged places. The first of these is the Virgin Mary. The Spirit dwelled within Mary, and raised her to the height of the divine: the one who was born of Mary shall be called the Son of God (Lk 1:35). We also witness the revelation of the Spirit in missioning. For example, the Spirit descends upon the disciples at Pentecost, and missions them to spread the gospel message among all peoples. The Spirit is further revealed in the gifts of members of the faith community. In community, many gifts and services come to the fore, and all of these come from the Holy Spirit.

The consummate revelation of the indwelling of the Spirit is Jesus. He is the one who is anointed by the Spirit to bring the good news to the poor and liberation to those who are in bondage. Jesus and the Spirit are interdependent. He is conceived by the Spirit (Mt 1:20; Lk 1:35), and at his baptism the Spirit descends upon him, and remains with him (Jn 1:32). He casts out demons in the power of the Spirit (Mt 12:28), and is himself raised from the dead by the same power (Rom 1:4). Jesus is filled with the Holy Spirit, and is thus the new human, fully free, and liberated from age-old bonds. In the power of the Spirit, he launches his messianic reign of liberation for all peoples:

> The Spirit of the Lord is upon me,
> because he has anointed me to bring good news to the poor.
> He has sent me to proclaim release to the captives
> and recovery of sight to the blind,
> to let the oppressed go free,
> to proclaim the year of the Lord's favour. (Lk 4:18–21)

The interdependence of Jesus and the Spirit in the New Testament is such that a test for the presence of the Spirit is whether or not it enables one to confess "Jesus is Lord." (1 Cor 12:3)

The Spirit Lives Within Us

Immediately before his betrayal and arrest, when Jesus knew that he would be leaving his disciples, he prays for them:

"I ask not only on behalf of these, but also on behalf of those who will believe in me through their word, that they may all be one. As you Father, are in me and I am in you, may they also be in us, so that the world may believe that you have sent me. The glory that you have given me I have given them, so that they may be one, as we are one, I in them and you in me, that they may become completely one, so that the world may know that you have sent me and have loved them even as you have loved me. Father, I desire that those also, whom you have given me, may be with me where I am, to see my glory, which you have given me because you loved me before the foundation of the world.

"Righteous Father, the world does not know you, but I know you; and these know that you have sent me. I made your name known to them, and I will make it known, so that the love with which you have loved me may be in them, and I in them." (Jn 17:20-26)

Jesus' promise is that the Spirit of God will come to dwell not simply *with* his disciples, but *within* them. They will continue to experience his presence and hear the truth of his message. This indwelling of the Holy Spirit is particularly evident in people's awareness of the gifts of the Spirit, in the early faith community (1 Cor 12–14), and in the understanding of baptism: "there are varieties of gifts, but the same Spirit" (1 Cor 12:4), and "For in the one Spirit we were all baptized into one body—Jews or Greeks, slaves or free—and we were all made to drink of one Spirit" (1 Cor 12:13). The Spirit is the gift of the Risen Lord, the power who teaches us the mind of Christ (1 Cor 2:16), the one who pours the love of God into our hearts (Rom 5:5), empowers our new life in Christ (Rom 8:11), and motivates and equips us for discipleship and service (Rom 8:14).

Such motivation is evident in how the spiritual gifts of the faithful are manifested and accepted in the community. In the scriptures, we witness many diverse gifts of the Spirit, each of which should be respected.

When we recognize and celebrate the diversity of spiritual gifts, we recognize our interdependence, and encourage mutual support. Paul reminds us, however, that the important gifts are not the sensational ones, such as speaking in tongues, but the gifts of faith, hope and, above all these, love. The primary criterion for life in the Spirit is an unconditional love of God and others, especially those who are marginalized. Such love is motivated by God's love. The test of the various gifts that the Spirit gives is whether they serve the common good, rather than causing division and contention in the community. A true gift of the Spirit builds up the whole community; it does not serve the self-aggrandizement of a few.

Beyond these spiritual gifts of the early faith community is a special outpouring of the Holy Spirit at Pentecost. The descent of the Spirit upon the disciples at Pentecost is not the first sign of the presence of the Spirit of God, nor is it the inauguration of the Christian community. Rather, it is the first fruits of God's saving action in the Risen Jesus, and a moment when the early faith community is empowered in a definite way. Pentecost means that the Spirit will never more be wholly withdrawn from the world. To fully understand Pentecost, we must recognize a major point: Christmas, Good Friday, Easter and Pentecost, all the great "once for all events" that we celebrate as Christians, are so closely interconnected that they represent the one and the same salvific event of God in human history. Pentecost is the culmination of Easter, and Easter is the glorification of the Risen Lord: "a glorification which includes his exaltation upon the cross, and his exaltation at the right hand of the Father in a single festival."[11]

On the day of Pentecost, when the Holy Spirit is made manifest, Peter delivers a speech to the people gathered before him. Interestingly, on this day when the Holy Spirit descends straight from above, Peter does not invite people to look upward, beyond their own time and history, to see if the Spirit is coming from a realm beyond them. Peter tells them, rather, to be baptized, because it is here and now, in the sacramental sign of baptism, that the Holy Spirit is present:

> "Repent, and be baptized every one of you in the name of Jesus Christ so that your sins may be forgiven; and you will receive the gift of the Holy Spirit. For the promise is for you, for your children, and for all who are far away, everyone whom the Lord our God calls to him." (Acts 2:38-39)

At Pentecost, the Holy Spirit becomes present to all believers. It is a time of transition from the mysterious, joyous events around Jesus' resurrection to an empowerment of all members of the Christian community who will enable this same belief in the presence of Jesus to manifest itself in history.

Pentecost fulfills Jesus' promise to his disciples. He recognized their sorrow at his departure, and he promised them another Advocate, one who would take what he had received from the Father and make it his own, one who would declare the gospel message to them, and who would be for them the Spirit of truth. The empowerment that the disciples receive is the person-gift of the Spirit of Jesus, the Son of God. The unfathomable mystery of Pentecost for the disciples is that God has bestowed upon all humanity the reality of God's own Spirit, and it is this personal presence of the Spirit as gift that continues the presence of Jesus within us. It draws us into the relationship that Jesus has with his Father, and, consequently, confers upon us a share in his ministry also. If we are in communion with Jesus because we have been given a share in his Spirit, then the Spirit is the closest divine Person to us. The work of the Spirit is to invite us to the Son, and to form us into sons and daughters of the Father. The personal presence of the Spirit that Jesus left with us guarantees that Jesus remains in us. The Holy Spirit is the one who invites us to the Son and the Father, and is the gift of our communion with Jesus. The Spirit creates a new life within us, and is the agent of our second birth. Just as we were first born from our mother's womb, so we must be born anew by the power of the Holy Spirit. The Spirit within us is the power of transformation from the old to the new, from enslavement to freedom, to a new life in communion with God. If we open ourselves to the presence of the Holy Spirit, then the Spirit will live in us, and so, too, will the Son and the Father, the Holy Trinity: God-within-us.

II.   We Are Spirit for the World

The new empowerment to act, by those who are filled with the Spirit, equips all members of the church community for significant service. Gifted by the same Spirit, all become contributors to the common good and equal partners in the continued creative and redemptive work of God in the world. The implications of this empowerment for ministry are obvious. The Spirit of God who was released through the earthly ministry of Jesus, who was united to and who transformed the humanity of Jesus, is now conferred upon us. We have now received the gift of the grace of the Holy Spirit for the purpose of divine and human communion: "When we cry, 'Abba! Father!' it is that very Spirit bearing witness with our spirit that we are children of God, and if children, then heirs, heirs of God and joint heirs with Christ—if, in fact, we suffer with him so that we may also be glorified with him" (Rom 8:15-17). If we are open to the presence of the Spirit within us, it will enrich us, and those around us.

The liberating experience of the Spirit is freely given to us in grace. Often we overlook it, sometimes we repress it, or do not take it seriously, but if we consider the times in our lives when we feel the fullness of freedom, or when we hope against all reason, then we will see the work of the Spirit. It is the Spirit who brings the work of Jesus to completion within each of us, and it is the Spirit who graces us with participation in the one life of the triune God: "Everything a person can say about the essence of glory and end of the Christian can be summed up by saying that he (or she) has received the Spirit of the Father, and in this way has been filled with the divine life. That exhausts everything else."[12]

Life in the Spirit is the pinnacle of theological anthropology, and the central characteristic of service and ministry. The Spirit is the Lord of Life and giver of liberty. The positive experience of the Spirit within us is vitalizing and liberating, and as we are liberated so we can liberate others. The Spirit within us is to be shared so that others may come to know such liberty, and the blessings of salvation, through our ministry. The only way in which we can share the Spirit is by living lives of shared communion. From the example of the Trinity, we are called to "perichoretic" living.

One Community in the Spirit

If the Christian God in its Trinity means three Persons in eternal communion, and we are created in the image of this triune God, then, we, too, are called to live in communion. We are image and likeness of the Trinity, and in our union with the Trinity as the interconnection of humanity and divinity, we are community beings. In imaging the Trinity we are called to maintain relationships of loving communion. Trinitarian theology is ultimately a theology of relationships: God to us, we to God, and we to each other. The doctrine of the Trinity affirms that the essence of God is relational. God exists as three divine Persons, united in a communion of freedom and love. God is love, and love requires community. The doctrine of the Trinity is the account of that community, and of sharing in the life of God. The power of the Spirit of God creates this community, and if we live in Christ, and by the power of the Holy Spirit, then we can be one community. The Spirit remakes us as persons-in-community who refuse to live as isolated, self-centred individuals. In community, each person is turned totally toward others. Everything is placed in common. Such is the sense of community that comes from the radical communion of the Trinity.

The Spirit of God brings about true communion—hypostatic union—of God and humanity. The Spirit humanizes God, and divinizes human beings, and this becomes a reality for us in our participation in the sacraments. La Cugna explains the sacramental dimension of the Trinity:

> In Baptism and chrismation (confirmation), the Spirit joins us to Jesus Christ, to his life and death, to his way of being with others, to his total reliance on God. In the Eucharist, we recall, give thanks for, and celebrate the true union of divine and human, and, as the bread and wine signify outwardly, we 'receive' into our bodies this communion. These sacraments of initiation are means by which the Spirit divinizes persons, incorporating us into the very life of God by uniting us with Jesus Christ.[13]

While the Spirit does not change human nature into divine nature, it brings about a union of God and human nature. The uniqueness of the Spirit's personhood is that it unites everyone and everything with God. This union conforms human beings to the person of Jesus and, as deified persons, we are able to enter into relationships with self, others, creation, and with God in a way that corresponds to Jesus' way of being in relationship. This is the essence of theological anthropology: the goal of human nature is to imitate the person of Jesus Christ who, in his hypostatic union, unites human and divine natures, and the Holy Spirit incorporates us into the life of the triune God, into the mystery of *perichoresis. Perichoresis* includes God and human persons in interpenetration. La Cugna points out that

> living as a person in communion, in right relationship, is the meaning of salvation and the ideal of Christian faith. God is interactive, neither solitary nor isolated. Human beings are created

in the image of the relational God and gradually are being perfected in that image (*theosis*), making more and more real the communion of all creatures with one another. The doctrine of the Trinity stresses the relational character of personhood over and against the reduction of personhood to a product of social relations. Thus it can serve as a critique of cultural norms of personhood, whether that of 'rugged individualism' or 'me first' morality, as well as patterns of inequality based on gender, race, ability, and so forth.[14]

The Greek term for the communion produced by the Holy Spirit is *koinonia*. *Koinonia* neither neutralizes the individual, nor obscures each person's uniqueness, nor takes away individual freedom in favour of a collective will. Rather, the goal of Christian community, understood as *koinonia*, is to provide a place where every single person is accepted in their unique and unrepeatable image of God, irrespective of their abilities or status. Our uniqueness is related to human freedom. Freedom means not independence and self-sufficiency, but being united with God in our image and likeness of God.

In this freedom we, as individuals, live out this Spirit of God. It is only within the context of *koinonia* that we can become who we are meant to be as image of God. Each person has the responsibility to maintain community by contributing his or her gifts for the good of all. It is only when we can relate and live in community that we are fully free, because it is from the equality of persons in community that each of us derives the dignity that we share as equal partners in the divine-human communion. The roles and expectations of the members of the community will certainly differ, but the worth and dignity of each is unconditional as equal partners before God. The criterion for evidence of the activity of the Spirit is whether or not genuine communion exists among persons.

It is from equality in the *koinonia* of the Spirit that one is led to *diakonia*, or ministry. *Diakonia* is the Greek word for service, and refers to all types of ministry, official or unofficial, that people perform for the church community.[15] *Koinonia* leads *everyone*, and not just a few, to *diakonia*, as members of the community constituted by the Spirit. Jürgen Moltmann reiterates this point:

> [I]t is not the monarchy of a ruler that corresponds to the triune God; it is the community of men and women without privileges

and without subjugation. The three divine Persons have everything in common except their personal characteristics. So the Trinity corresponds to a community in which people are defined through their relations with one another, not in opposition to one another, in terms of power and possession.[16]

Koinonia is the foundation of ministry. We are all joined in Jesus by the Spirit who is the gift not only to individual believers but, above all, to the faith community. In community, individual believers become a "WE" united in the Spirit working within us. A theology of the Spirit affirms the fundamental insights that the entire church community exists in a continual state of *epiclesis* (Spirit invocation), and that all of the baptized are called to exercise this ministry. This is what we mean when we talk about a person's *charism*. Charism is not simply a specific talent or apostolate. Charism goes much deeper than this. Charism comes from the Greek word *charis*, meaning "grace"; *charism* is the free gift of grace. Grace is the self-donation of the presence of God in the Person of the Holy Spirit. It is the one Spirit, given as a gift to all of us, who is the source of the varieties of ministries among believers. When we share our charism with those around us in our ministry, we are ultimately sharing the gift of the Holy Spirit. We begin to mediate, or put into action, the grace that has been given to us. In this activity, we begin to witness the effects of Pentecost.

Koinonia is lived when Christians are true to their trinitarian heritage. We are urged to live in community because that is the way our triune God really is. Thus, contrary to its reputation as an incomprehensible teaching, the doctrine of the Trinity is the most practical and relevant of all Christian doctrines. It is a doctrine that shows Christians how to live their lives: in *koinonia* and *diakonia*, as equal members of a community created in the image of God and who are dedicated to the service of one another. The trinitarian conception of God is revolutionary for one's own self-understanding as a person, for the church as a community, and for all those who minister in this community.

Chapter 5

Sacramental Theology:
The Sacramentality of Our Lives

*Jesus said to them, "I am the bread of life. Whoever comes to me will never
be hungry, and whoever believes in me will never be thirsty." (Jn 6:35)*

Introduction

The recognition of the human person as created in the image of
God, and the challenge of discipleship, are celebrated and
strengthened in the sacramental life of the church community, especially
in the sacraments of baptism and Eucharist. Baptism initiates us into the
Christian community, and the Eucharist nourishes and sustains us as we
strive to live out the challenge of our discipleship. The foundation of
who we are as individuals, and what we share as a community, is most
evident in these two sacraments. Baptism and Eucharist are the primary
sacraments of ministry and community. Our challenge is to embrace the
sacred mentality of people who have answered Jesus' call to conversion
and discipleship in baptism, and to live as a eucharistic community of
disciples.

The sacraments support and celebrate the definitive moments in a
Christian's life: birth, belonging, forgiveness, reconciliation, thanksgiving,
vocation, sickness, death, and resurrection. They express, and bring
meaning to, important times in the lives of believers, which, in and of
themselves, can otherwise be ambivalent experiences for us. While we
can never be sure exactly how the sacraments operate in our lives, or
how God's grace is actually working in our lives, we do know that every

way in which God relates to us is grounded in human experience. We also know that Jesus is the one who has broken into our reality and imbued this experience with the divine. The sacraments operate within Jesus' relationship to humanity, and are the external expressions of Jesus' continued presence in our lives. Christian faith claims that God's saving work in Jesus Christ has heightened the sacramentality of life and that the Holy Spirit continues Jesus' sacramental effect throughout human history. Groome describes it this way:

> Understood within the sacramentality of life in the world, the seven sacraments are sacred symbols that mediate God's grace in Jesus with heightened effect. This they do by the power of the Holy Spirit working through the Christian community. Each sacrament is a way of encountering the Risen Christ and of receiving the particular grace that the sacrament symbolizes, be that of initiating, empowering, sustaining, forgiving, healing, serving, or bonding. But Catholic Christians should never think of the seven sacraments apart from life.[1]

The meaning and practice of the sacraments rest upon the integral relationship between christology and theological anthropology—between the Incarnation of Jesus and the incarnate reality of our lives. The hypostatic union, and the self-transcendence of humanity, relate the Body of Christ to the laws of historical human existence. In other words, the meaning and effective celebration of the sacraments take into account the principles that underlie all humanizing celebrations of life. Liturgical practice is never separated from human life.

We are incarnate beings, and therefore can express ourselves as persons only in the reality of our body. Edward Kilmartin notes that anthropology describes the human body as the most original expression of the individual:

> The body is the most original appearance and source of self-knowledge; it is not static. It grows, waxes, wanes, and succumbs. In this process particular junctures of biological life become sources of new self-understandings. There are situations such as puberty and aging which cannot be manipulated but only accepted as inevitable stages. They can be called boundary situations because despite the freedom which a human being experiences to make changes and to manipulate things and

people, they reveal the weakness of a person to overtake and master oneself. In short, they manifest the finitude of the human being and so raise the question of the meaning of life.[2]

While anthropology does not deal with sacraments in such a specific way, some of its findings correspond to the ways in which sacraments operate in our lives. Sacramental expression and activity correspond to the nature of human beings. The human person is "spirit in body," a being that develops through contact with the surrounding environment and with other people. That the human spirit expresses itself in bodiliness has obvious implications for the sacraments.[3] The sacraments are inseparable from human experience. They relate to our humanity and thereby honour the greatest embodied event in human history: the Incarnation. Sacramental rites refer to the fundamental sacramental meaning of the human condition.[4]

Sacramental theology does not, therefore, confine itself to a purely anthropological explanation for understanding the sacraments. Rather, it moves to a theological anthropology by tracing the sacramentality of the Christian life back to Jesus Christ. The gospels show that Jesus was aware of the defining moments in people's lives. He was conscious of their deep longings, their need for personal contact and a supportive community, and their search for meaning in their lives. The relationships and actions of Jesus' life, death, and resurrection—the Paschal mystery—fulfill these needs; in these relationships and actions we find the meaning of the sacraments. The Paschal mystery gives the sacraments meaning *for us*, but this mystery is Jesus' own life, *his* defining moments. As the essential expression of who God is for us and in our salvation, Jesus brings meaning to Christian life and faith.[5] The sacraments are founded on the Incarnation itself, and on the preaching and actions of Jesus. Jesus infuses the everyday reality of our lives with new meaning. He sanctified defining moments in his followers' lives by giving them a meaning that is continued in the celebration of the sacraments. The sacraments show different ways in which Christians are integrated into the mystery of Jesus Christ, and they awaken the awareness that each person shares with others in the pilgrimage of the People of God.

The sacraments are therefore "paradigms for the whole range of possible instances of relating the Word of God to concrete situations of life."[6] Through participation in the sacraments, each believer moves from one stage of human life to the next within, and supported by, the community of faith. The sacraments are also individual invitations. Apart from the Eucharist, in which the sacrament of the Body of Christ is intended to be shared with all participants, all other celebrations are for the specific believer, in which a proclamation of the personal offer of God's grace is directed to each person. The community shares in this celebration by agreement and witness to the grace being offered to one of its members. The community is also renewed by its members' witness and by its participation in this moment. In this way, the community recognizes responsibility toward the individual recipient of the sacrament, and also receives spiritual help to support the individual's growth in the life of faith.

I.   Symbol and Sacrament

How do the sacraments render meaning in our lives? An answer to this question requires some discussion of symbols. Symbols are an important part of the ways in which people communicate. We cannot relate to another person without some form of symbolic expression, such as the language we use to communicate with one another. The reality of our existence unfolds in symbolic expression. Symbolic expression requires relationship. To say that our own existence is symbolic is to say that the fullness of our humanity draws us into relationships of communication.

While symbols are an integral part of human reality, what we think and say can never be perfectly clear. The symbols of a handshake or a hug, for example, can say many things, and can describe what is going on, yet they cannot completely define what is really happening. Metaphors and artistic forms help us to share with one another what cannot be expressed in words, but which can be understood. Symbols are connected to recognition, understanding, and communication, and help us to communicate shared values and meanings. Symbols take us beyond instinct and natural reflex. This is the difference between instinctive behaviour, such as a blink, and symbolic expression, such as a wink.

Humans are symbol-making and symbol-using beings, and, because of this, we are able to form community. A symbol never simply points to a reality beyond itself, like a stop sign, for example. A symbol contains the reality that it symbolizes. Real symbols are not *linked to* our reality, they *constitute* our reality. A symbol *does* what it symbolizes. Symbols are integral to how we relate to one another, and all beings are, therefore, necessarily symbolic. This is the central theme of Rahner's article "The Theology of Symbol," in which he states that "all beings are by their nature symbolic because they necessarily 'express' themselves in order to attain their own nature."[7] When we express ourselves, each of us is displaying our human nature. Our embodiment does not just point to who we are; in its symbolic expression, it is the reality of who we are. Similarly, the symbol of the bread and wine of the Eucharist does not just point to the real presence of the Body and Blood of Jesus; in its symbolic reality, it *is* his presence.

When a group of people want to communicate their sense of the sacred, symbols are especially evident: symbol and sacrament are inseparable. The sacraments are best described as symbolic actions that mediate the presence of God. The Holy Spirit uses our human actions to make Jesus Christ, with his historically unique saving activity, actually present to us. Symbol signifies mystery, and when the sacramental symbol is being performed, God is making known God's hidden, saving presence. God's self-communication is made historically tangible in the form of the symbol. A sacrament is thus a cause of God's grace, provided that we believe grace is conferred on account of the sacramental symbol. Sacraments actualize our inner capacity for God, who is always disclosed mysteriously and symbolically. To live this sacramentality is to live the Paschal Mystery. By living the sacramentality of the Paschal mystery, Christians bring meaning to their shared lives. Since this mystery is centred on the life, death, and resurrection of Jesus, the shared meaning that manifests itself is the life of loving service and discipleship.

We express the fullness of our human nature in relationships, and relationships flourish in community. Sacraments have a strong communal component to them, and in the life of the Christian, this communal component is the church community. Sacraments are a daily challenge for the church community because they draw its faith into action by calling the community to be what each of the sacraments symbolizes.[8]

What Is a Sacrament?

Sacramental theology answers the question "What is a sacrament?" If theology is about God, then sacramental theology is about humanity's response to God's grace and presence in our lives, and examines how this response affects our faith. Rahner summarizes this point when he says:

Insofar as fundamental theology presupposes dogmatic theology as its foundation, it is not only reasonable, but necessary to speak of fundamental sacramental theology. This would be a theology of symbolism in general derived from a study of [humanity].[9]

On a general level, sacramentality involves three major elements: 1) the meaning of human experience; 2) the saving presence of God in our lives; and 3) the transforming effect of human beings, both individually and communally, because of the presence of God in their lives. The sacraments empower humanity to live in right relationship with God, with self, and with others, which is where sacramental grace is most evident, and where God's presence and action are manifested. The sacraments are not human inventions to summon God at our convenience. They can never be a way of controlling God, or a magical way of conjuring up God's presence. In the sacraments, it is God who calls us, and we who respond to God's initiative.

It is difficult to give a satisfactory definition of a sacrament because there is no general sacrament, but, rather, concrete individual sacraments. In broad terms, a sacrament is an external rite, or symbol, that in some way conveys grace to the believer. The term "sacrament" is a Latin translation of the Greek word *mysterion,* which means mystery, or a secret, once hidden, but now revealed by God. For Christians, it means the hidden plan of God revealed in Jesus Christ. In New Testament theology, *mysterion* denotes the realization and revelation of God's plan of salvation:

> In former generations this mystery was not made known to humankind, as it has now been revealed to his holy apostles and prophets by the Spirit: that is, the Gentiles have become fellow heirs, members of the same body, and sharers in the promise in Christ Jesus through the gospel. (Eph 3:5-6)

For Paul, the sacraments are a way of living out the Pasch, the great Christian festival of redemption that was a continuation of the Jewish Passover and Exodus. The Pasch was a commemoration of both the crucifixion and the resurrection of Jesus. The sacraments link us with Jesus' death in order to allow us to partake in his resurrection. In Matthew, Jesus gives the sacramental rites as a sign of his presence in the faith community, and he associates the forgiveness of sins with baptism and Eucharist. For Luke, it is the Holy Spirit who accompanies the work of the community and makes it fruitful. The Spirit ensures that the gospel is successfully proclaimed and leaves a mark in the community of believers. This belief is expressed in the rites of baptism, in the breaking of the bread, and in the laying on of hands. In John, baptism and Eucharist make us partakers of the true life of the Word that came among us to reveal the mystery of God and to lead us to God.

The Latin term *sacramentum,* while based on this scriptural understanding of *mysterion,* has a juridical meaning of oath or allegiance. *Sacramentum* has two original meanings:

1. It was a legal term for money that was dedicated to the deity from a person who lost a trial.

2. It referred to the action by which a soldier committed himself in taking an oath to his leader and to the emperor. Sometimes he was even branded with a sign of the general he was to serve.

Tertullian employed the sense of commitment by oath when he translated the Greek *mysterion* as *sacramentum* in describing baptism as a permanent consecration to God's service through word (oath) and visible sign (brand), made possible by sharing in the Paschal Mystery of Jesus' life, death, and resurrection.

From these interpretations, Augustine developed the concept of *mysterion/sacramentum* that was influential in the writings of later theologians.[10] He describes a sacrament as a "sacred sign," or "visible word," composed of word and material element: that is, the words of the sacramental rite and the symbol used. Later theologians, especially Aquinas, developed the distinction between the matter (the material substance) and the form (the verbal formula) of the sacraments. Augustine developed his theory of the sacraments in the context of his interpretation of the New Testament in the light of neo-Platonic philosophical thought. He placed *sacramentum* in the category of *signa,* visible signs representing an invisible reality. A *sacramentum* is a sacred sign *(sacrum signum),* that is, a sign designated by God to point to a divine reality *(res divina).* The sign contains this sacred reality within itself. Augustine's ideas dominated pre-scholastic thought. The *sacramentum* came to be understood as "the visible form of the invisible grace of God" *(invisibilis gratiae visibilis forma).* Most Catholics learn this in the catechism definition of a sacrament as "an outward sign of invisible grace," or "an outward sign, instituted by

Christ, to give grace." The latter definition was formulated in the scholastic period of the eleventh to the twelfth centuries.

In the scholastic period, a new systematic approach to the sacraments was introduced, influenced by a renewed interest in Aristotle's philosophy. The concern of the time was to distinguish the principal ways in which God builds up the church and brings it to salvation.[11] This era distinguished the seven sacraments from sacramentals, such as holy water or a crucifix, which were understood to lack the guarantee of grace associated with the seven sacraments. The seven sacraments were affirmed as the principal causes of grace, and the means by which God chooses to sanctify humanity and unify the church. The church's present list of seven sacraments dates from this period, as does the aforementioned definition of a sacrament as "an outward sign, instituted by Christ, to give grace."

"Sacrament" had a broader meaning prior to the twelfth century. The sense of the Greek word *mysterion* was used originally to name any manifestation of God's power and love in space and time. Such a broad definition does not describe what the particular sacraments are, but neither can we reduce the participation of God's grace in our lives to a juridical oath. In sacramental theology there are two extremes to avoid:

1. The sacraments are important because they are the only means to receive God's grace. In this instance, ritual minimalism becomes the norm, and sacraments are separated from the broader context of life in creation.

2. Since God is in all life and creation, we do not need the sacraments. In this instance, communal worship and ritual celebration are eliminated.

Vatican II proposed a balance between these two extremes. Strongly influenced by the insights of modern liturgical scholars[12] and systematic theologians, it challenges us to look more deeply at the relationship between how we live our faith and our understanding of what the sacraments represent for us. The Constitution on the Sacred Liturgy (*Sacrosanctum Concilium*) states:

> The purpose of the sacraments is to sanctify [humanity], to build up the Body of Christ, and finally to give worship to God. Because they are signs they also instruct. They not only presuppose faith, but by words and objects they also nourish, strengthen, and express

it; that is why they are called 'sacraments of faith.' They do indeed impart grace, but in addition, the very act of celebrating them disposes the faithful more effectively to receive this grace in a fruitful manner to worship God daily, and to practice charity.

It is therefore of capital importance that the faithful easily understand the sacramental signs and with great eagerness have frequent recourse to those sacraments which were instituted to nourish the Christian life. (*SC* 59)

While the seven sacraments celebrate and sanctify defining experiences in our lives, the grace of these experiences must be continually strengthened by acknowledging the sacredness of all life and creation. Groome refers to this as the "sacramental principle," and places the seven sacraments within this context. The sacramental principle proposes that everything in our life-world can be a "visible sign of invisible grace," or as St. Ignatius of Loyola says, Christians are invited to "see God in all things."[13]

Jesus: "Primordial" Sacrament

Two major themes in contemporary sacramental theology are Jesus as "Primordial" Sacrament, and the Church as "Fundamental" Sacrament.[14] Regarding the first, Ray Noll states that "If you want to know what a sacrament is and what a sacrament does you can do no better than look at Jesus as we find him in the New Testament."[15] It is from the Word of God, taking flesh in the person of Jesus Christ, in living, suffering, dying, and rising again, that all sacraments derive their power. Jesus is the first, or primordial, sacrament, since he mediates God's presence in the world.[16] This mediation is continued in our earthly life by the sacraments that re-present Jesus to us. Jesus, as primordial sacrament, rests upon the New Testament theology of *mysterion*. In Ephesians and Colossians, *mysterion* refers not only to something secret or hidden, but also to the revelation of God's saving intent in Jesus Christ. Many early church writers, including Augustine, called Jesus the *mysterion Dei*. In the Latin translation of the Bible, the word *mysterion* is given as *sacramentum*, and so it was natural to call Jesus the *sacramentum Dei*.[17] To discover Jesus as the sacrament of God is to recognize what was unique about the event of Jesus of Nazareth. The heart of the first disciples' witness is faith in Jesus' resurrection and the certainty of his continued presence. To live in his presence is to understand what the sacraments are all about. However,

Jesus is not just a man who signifies God, he *is* the presence of God: he embodies God. Therefore, Jesus defines the sacraments. We do not use our definition of sacraments, or our approach to sacramental theology, to define Jesus' identity. Everything the sacraments are flows from who he is.

The New Testament witness to the events of Jesus' life and his dealings with people shows how much he was, in his very person, a sign, a "making visible of the presence of God." Everything that he did had a sacramental character, that is, the ability to make God present. The christological dogma of the Council of Chalcedon (425) includes an understanding of Jesus as sacrament: "The most intimate closeness of God (God's essence, uncreated grace) and receptive human nature as its real symbol (effective sign) are present in Jesus, unseparated and without confusion."[18] Precisely because the saving acts of the human Jesus are performed by a divine person, they have a divine power to save, and because this divine power to save appears in visible form, Jesus' saving activity is sacramental. Schillebeeckx concludes:

> The man Jesus as the personal visible realization of the divine grace of redemption is *the* sacrament, the primordial sacrament, because this man, the Son of God himself, is intended by the father to be in his humanity the only way to the actuality of redemption.[19]

In his understanding of Jesus as primordial sacrament, Schillebeeckx was instrumental in developing a sacramental theology that was faithful to the insights of Aquinas, yet free of the minimalist tendency of late scholasticism. His method was to look, not to Aristotelian philosophy, but to contemporary existentialism with its grounding in human experience. For Schillebeeckx, the essence of a sacramental experience is an encounter between persons. When two persons encounter one another deeply, they discover something of the mystery of what the other is. Sacraments are outward signs that reveal a transcendent reality— a divine reality. When people encountered Jesus, they encountered the mystery of God. Even after his death, Jesus remained a sacrament to those who accepted his message and believed in him. In his resurrection, he revealed that the mystery believers saw in him, and the mystery of the God they believed in, were one and the same. Similarly, even after Jesus was gone, they continued to sense the presence of that mystery. Those who believed in Jesus, who were called together as a community in his name, became sacraments to others. Through their actions, rooted in Jesus' message of love and forgiveness, Jesus himself acted. The early faith community recognized its complete dependence on Jesus as it was being formed by the Holy Spirit into an instrument of his continuing presence.

The Church: Fundamental Sacrament

The sacramental witness of the early faith community continues today in the church. *Lumen Gentium* of Vatican II attests to this sacramental nature of the church:

> By her relationship with Christ, the church is a kind of sacrament of intimate union with God, and of the unity of all [humankind], that is, she is a sign and an instrument of such union and unity. (*LG* 1)

> The term 'sacrament' is here applied to the church by analogy with the seven sacraments properly so-called, which are particular actions of Christ in and through the church. The church itself is a sort of 'general sacrament,' a grace, as the constitution here explains, it is a 'sign' and instrument which unites [us] supernaturally to God and to one another.[20]

The church is the fundamental sacrament in the sense of making Jesus present to the world, and it will continue to be effective as long as it manifests this redemptive work of Jesus. It does so by virtue of the fact that it is the Body of Christ. What was visible in Jesus has now passed over into the sacrament of the church. But the church does not replace Jesus in his absence; Jesus is still with us. The church is what it is because of its dependence on Jesus, and because Jesus' Spirit is present within it. The church must, therefore, be understood relationally, that is, in relationship to the one true author of salvation, Jesus Christ, in the Holy Spirit, according to the will of God. In this regard, Vorgrimler believes that Vatican II's

> unwillingness to locate the foundation of human salvation in the church is the reason for its avoidance of a conscious application of the term 'primordial' sacrament to the church. Instead, it pointed to the simple analogy, that is, similarity in a still greater difference, between the mystery of Jesus Christ, and the mystery of the church, between the humanity of Jesus, and

the visible form of the church (*LG* 8) in order to direct attention to the limits of a sacramental ecclesiology.[21]

While we note the difference, we acknowledge that the church is the contemporary presence of God's salvific will in the world. The church is the sign, the abiding presence of the primordial sacramental word of definitive grace that Jesus Christ is in the world. As the enduring presence of Jesus, the church is the fundamental sacrament, a wellspring for the other sacraments: "From Christ, the church has an intrinsically sacramental nature."[22] Jesus Christ's abiding presence in the church is the sign that God, in love, identifies Godself in Jesus with the world, and because it is the sign of the grace of God in the world in Jesus Christ, this sign can never become a meaningless symbol. The sacraments, as official signs and acts of the church, are also signs and acts of Jesus. They signify the continued redemptive action of Jesus Christ for us.

II: Baptism and Eucharist:
The Sacramental Foundations of Ministry

Baptism is the first and fundamental sacrament. It is the sacrament of purification, sanctification, and rebirth (Jn 3:1-5). We are reborn in the Spirit and grace of Jesus Christ, and like all of the sacraments, this is an action of God, and not of human initiative. Baptism is the means by which a person attains the fullness of baptismal grace: a new life conformed to the death and resurrection of Jesus Christ, together with the remission of all sin. It mediates that life which God, through God's self-communication, bestows upon human beings for eternal life. An understanding of baptism follows from an understanding of our triune God, and how God communicates with us in Jesus Christ.

The word "baptism" comes from the Greek *baptizein,* which means to immerse. Rather than having a small amount of water poured on their forehead, those being baptized originally walked into large cisterns, which were often in the shape of a cross. They went down one side by a series of steps, totally immersed themselves, and came out the other side. This total immersion symbolized that baptism is both immersion into the death of Jesus, and also a resurrection.

Christian baptism is in continuity with the baptism "of repentance for the forgiveness of sins" (Mk 1:4) practised by John the Baptist. The symbolism of immersion, with its implication of danger, the resolve to repent, to orient oneself to the will of God, and to work for the reign of God, are all elements of John's baptism retained in the Christian rite. It was of decisive importance for the early Christian community that Jesus had been baptized by John. In asking John to baptize him, Jesus showed solidarity with the people among whom he lived and worked in Judea and Jerusalem. Or, in relationship to its importance for sacramental theology, Vorgrimler states: it "acknowledged that he regarded the external demonstration of an internal disposition by means of a symbolic action proper and important."[23] The authorization and continued practice of baptism is often placed in the command of Jesus to "Go therefore and make disciples of all nations, baptizing them in the name of the Father and of the Son and of the Holy Spirit, and teaching them to obey everything that I have commanded you" (Mt 28:19-20). There is no doubt whatsoever about the importance of this command. Equally important is the fact that Jesus not only commanded baptism, but participated in the act by freely submitting himself to baptism by John.

Jesus' baptism also marked his vocation. Being a disciple of the Baptist, being a messianic prophet, being the Messiah himself, were successive elements in Jesus' understanding of his vocation. The glory of his baptism, where it points to Jesus as the Christ, the Son of God, implies the fullness of his humanity as one who responds to God's call, and to his commitment. At baptism he begins his ministry of love and service that will eventually lead to his death and resurrection. Jesus also gave John's baptism a meaning that it did not already have: a baptism for the *forgiveness* of sins. By entering into the waters of the Jordan, Jesus immersed all humanity. To this he adds a sense of filiation. Baptism is therefore integrally linked to revelation, a point the gospel writers stressed when they recorded the baptism of Jesus. The scene of Jesus' baptism is supplemented by a revelation scene:

> And when Jesus had been baptized, just as he came up from the water, suddenly the heavens were opened to him and he saw the Spirit of God descending like a dove and alighting on him. And a voice from heaven said, "This is my Son, the Beloved, with whom I am well pleased." (Mt 3:16-17)

The Holy Spirit descends upon Jesus, and his mission is made known to him. This scene does not deny that Jesus was always in the power of the Spirit before his baptism, and that he was aware of his mission to serve the reign of God and to do the Father's will. Such is also the case with us: the Holy Spirit is at work in our lives before baptism. It is the work of the Spirit that draws us to repentance and conversion. Our call to initiation is the initiative of God's grace, through the Holy Spirit, at work in our lives. All baptized persons are marked with a seal, and the first installment of their inheritance as sons and daughters of God is implanted in their hearts. The phrase "You are my Son, the Beloved" (Mk 1:11) shows that God recognized the eternal Son in the human Jesus. It also points to the belief that Jesus is the messiah, the one sent by God. Jesus is now able to begin his public life, the true baptism of his Pasch, in which he is immersed in death, and is risen to new life.

Jesus did not need to participate in a baptism of repentance and conversion, but by doing so he showed his solidarity with lost humanity. In this solidarity with sinners, Jesus fulfills all righteousness, so that those who are baptized are no longer slaves to sin, but are free. Baptism fully identifies us with Jesus' death. We are buried with him, and raised with him here and now. We live a new life in the power of the resurrection, and are confident that we will ultimately be one with him in a resurrection like his (Rom 6:3-11; Col 2:12; 3:1; Eph 2:5-6).[24]

Jesus uses the image of baptism when he relates the life of his disciples to his own mission of love: "Are you able to drink the cup that I drink, or be baptized with the baptism that I am baptized with?" (Mk 10:38), and Paul explains baptism within this context:

> Do you know that all of us who have been baptized into Christ Jesus were baptized into his death? Therefore we have been buried with him by baptism into death, so that, just as Christ was raised from the dead by the glory of the Father, so we too might walk in newness of life. (Rom 6:3-4)

Other images in the New Testament unfold the meaning of baptism:

> [Baptism is] a washing away of sin (1 Cor 6:11); a new birth (Jn 3:5); an enlightenment by Christ (5:14); a reclothing in Christ (Gal 3:27); a renewal by the Spirit (Titus 3:5); the experience of salvation from the flood (1 Cor 10:1-2); and a liberation into a new humanity in which barriers of division whether of sex, or race, or social status are transcended. (Gal 3:27-28; 1 Cor 12:15). The images are many but the reality is one.[25]

Baptism marks the beginning of the Christian's participation in the life, death, and resurrection of Jesus. It symbolizes one's death to an old way of life into a new life in Jesus Christ. When a person is initiated into the church community, they begin a journey that helps them to enter more fully into their baptismal identity. They are drawn into the love and life of the triune God, in whose name they are baptized. It is a symbol of our common discipleship. Through baptism we are brought into union with Jesus and with one another, and into the church.

Baptism recognizes the fullness of our humanity, and is Jesus' invitation to each one of us to enter into a relationship with God. It initiates us into our life of discipleship in Jesus Christ, and is an initial call to ministry. Through baptism Christians are initiated into the life of the church, and into the Paschal Mystery of Jesus Christ. Baptism is the first symbolic action of the church in a Christian's life. It symbolizes the human experience of relationship, community, belonging, and vocation. We understand baptism only to the extent that we understand Christianity and the church. It is inseparably linked to the Christian church community. Baptism is the community's way of marking the journey of faith and discipleship that will last throughout one's entire life. Its purpose is to initiate people into a life of discipleship in Jesus Christ, and to witness to the reign of God. In a narrow sense, baptism consists in the beginning of the Christian way of life and entry into the church community, but in a broader sense, it encompasses the whole life of Christian discipleship. It requires the ongoing commitment of the one who is baptized to witness to their faith, not just in word, but in action. It calls the person to live the unity of the love of God, and the love of human beings in following Jesus, and in the service of justice. Baptism, then, is not simply a one-time initiation into an institution, or some sort of Christian registry of church affiliation. It is, rather, an entrance into a relationship with Jesus Christ, and the conversion to, and acceptance of, a way of life dedicated to gospel discipleship.

The Institution of the Eucharist: Jesus said...

> "This is my body that is for you. Do this in remembrance of me." In the same way, he took the cup also, after supper, saying, "This cup is the new covenant in my blood. Do this, as often as you drink it, in remembrance of me." (1 Cor 11:24-25)

In the Eucharist the community of baptized disciples comes together to celebrate its unity in Jesus Christ. Through the grace of God in Jesus and the Holy Spirit, a person is initiated into this community of disciples, and through the same grace of God in the Eucharist, the person is sustained and nourished for the journey of discipleship. Baptism confirms our solidarity with Jesus and with others in conversion and forgiveness of sins, and the Eucharist is the continued sign of God's grace that gives life to the community and strengthens it for service in the world. Through participation in the Eucharist, people share the community's faith in an ever-deepening way. The faith in which they grow is their personal relationship and encounter with the Risen Jesus. In the eucharistic liturgy, people are led toward an ever-closer relationship with Jesus. This relationship interacts with everything else in their lives. It gives a new meaning to everything they are, and everything that they do. The Eucharist is a life-changing experience for both individuals and the community. Groome captures this concept when he states:

> Eucharist symbolizes all that reflects vitality and responsibility, peace, justice, care, and compassion—everything that fulfils the covenant—as it celebrates the *real* presence of the Risen Christ, makes 'an offering of praise' to God, bonds Christian community, sustains them with the 'bread of life' and empowers them for 'the life of the world.' (John 6:51) Eucharist is the 'sacrament of sacraments' (Aquinas' phrase)—for Christian faith, the most eminent instance of divine-human encounter.[26]

The words and actions of Jesus at the institution of the Eucharist are the heart of the celebration. The Eucharist is the sacrament of the Body and Blood of Jesus Christ. It is the sacrament of his real presence. The Eucharist is the centre of the sacramental life of the church community. Here, by the power of the Holy Spirit, the community encounters the Risen Jesus. The most important New Testament witnesses to the Eucharist are the accounts of the Last Supper (Mt 26:26-29; Mk 14:22-25; Lk 22:19-20; Jn 6:51-58; Acts 2:42; 1 Cor 11:24-25). These readings make it possible to reconstruct Jesus' final meal. Jesus gave his "Body" and "Blood" to be eaten and drunk under the appearances of bread and wine. He knows that he is going to die. He also understands the meal as anticipating the end of time, and the joy that will be celebrated then. Community is also important: Jesus is celebrating this meal with his friends, his disciples.

"Eucharist" comes from the Greek word *eucharistein,* which means "to give thanks." It is, literally, the thanks of one who has received "goodly gifts," and who, consequently, is thankful. The etymology of "eucharist" makes this more evident. *Eu* means "well" or "good," as in "euphoria," and *charis* means "gift." To say "eucharist" is therefore to say "the gift that you have given me is good."[27] The use of the word, however, comes from the liturgies of the Temple in Jerusalem. In the time before Jesus, it denoted the most important point of sacrifices, the climax of the "sacrifice of praise." For a long time, the prophets had been looking for a more spiritual dimension to the sacrifice, rather than the burning of sheep and oxen: "'For I desire steadfast love and not sacrifice,' says God, 'the knowledge of God rather than burnt offerings'" (Hos 6:6; cf. Mt 9:13; 12:7). After the return from exile, perhaps influenced·by the highly spiritual Persian religion, a custom was introduced to the Temple of accompanying the act of sacrifice with an act of thanksgiving. This thanksgiving became a ritual action that included a proclamation of the work of salvation accomplished by God. Eventually, this thanksgiving became the most important part of the sacrificial process. Beguerie explains:

> It was more vital than the animal or vegetable offering. In Hebrew it was called *todah*, and the Greek bible translated this word as *eucharista*. So when the gospel says that Jesus 'gives thanks,' it clearly means that this Last Supper of the Lord is the true sacrifice of praise.[28]

Thus, as directly instituted by Jesus, and in which his Body and Blood are truly present under the symbols of bread and wine, the Eucharist is in the fullest sense of the term a sacrament.[29] The actual sacramental symbols of the Eucharist are those of a meal: when bread, basic food, is distributed, it expresses a communal sharing, as does the wine, which also symbolizes joy and shared fullness of life. All of the meals that Jesus is recorded sharing during his earthly ministry proclaim the nearness of the reign of God. In his last meal, the nearness of this reign was connected to the immanence of his own death. After the resurrection, his presence is made known to his disciples in the breaking of the bread, and the Eucharist continues these meals of Jesus always as a sign of God's reign. The Eucharist is, then, a special kind of meal; a meal of thanksgiving, blessing, and sacrifice. It is a memorial, an *anamnesis*, of the suffering, death, and resurrection of Jesus: Christ has died, Christ is risen, Christ will come again. The Eucharist also looks to the future;

past and future are truly and effectively present in the real presence of Jesus himself. In the memorial of the Eucharist, we have the memorial of the living and effective symbol of Jesus' sacrifice, accomplished once and for all on the cross, and which is still operative today. Jesus Christ himself, with all that he has accomplished for us, is present in this *anamnesis,* granting us full communion with himself. This memorial that we celebrate is also an offer of ourselves as a living sacrifice in our daily lives. We offer ourselves to God, and are nourished, sanctified, and reconciled, so that we can be nourishment and reconciliation for those around us.

"Take this and divide it among yourselves..."

It is no accident that on the night he knew of his impending death, Jesus celebrated in community with his disciples. The Eucharist established a communion between Jesus and the participants in the eucharistic meal: a reciprocal indwelling in each other (Jn 6:51-58). Jesus gave of himself, and because of this self-giving sacrifice, he is bestowed with God's gift of eternal life. It is the same eternal life that is bestowed on us in our sharing in the Eucharist. When we receive the Body of Christ, we receive "ourselves," that true image of ourselves, in order to become more freely what we ought to be: the Body of Christ. The effect of this communion of Jesus with us is our unity with one another: "Because there is one bread, we who are many are one body, for we all partake of the one bread" (1 Cor 10:17). Our union with Jesus Christ creates community with those who are being nourished with this same Body of Christ. This means that the faith community shares in the Eucharist's effects, and these affect our everyday lives.

Vatican II emphasized the communal aspect of the Eucharist when it stated that Jesus is present, not only in the liturgical actions and in the sacrifice of the Eucharist, but also in the gathered community of believers. The effect of the Eucharist is not, therefore, purely personal, occurring only in the individual—although this is certainly relevant to how we as individuals live out the challenge of the Eucharist in our lives—but above all communal. In the Eucharist, God's gracious salvific will for all people and, most importantly, in all people, becomes present, tangible, and visible. The result is that the tangible, visible community of the faithful becomes that symbol that does not simply point to the grace and salvific will of God, but *is* the tangibility and permanence of this grace and of salvation. In the Eucharist the community of God's people is fully manifested. The ramifications of this are powerfully emphasized in the document by the World Council of Churches, *Baptism, Eucharist and Ministry*:

> The Eucharistic celebration demands reconciliation and sharing among all those regarded as brothers and sisters in the family of God and is a constant challenge in the search for appropriate relationships in social, economic, and political life. (Mt 5:23f; 1 Cor 10:16; 1 Cor 11:20-22; Gal 3:28) All kinds of injustice, racism, separatism, and lack of freedoms are radically challenged when we share in the body and blood of Christ. Through the Eucharist, the all-renewing grace of God penetrates and restores human personality and dignity....As participants in the Eucharist, therefore, we prove inconsistent if we are not actively participating in this ongoing restoration of the world's situation and the human condition.[30]

The Eucharist is, therefore, about solidarity in communion. All aspects of the rite, the mutual forgiveness of sins, the sign of peace, intercessions, eating and drinking together, taking the Eucharist to the sick and homebound, are all related to Jesus' own servanthood, and the discipleship that Christians profess: "The place of such ministry between the table and the needy properly testifies to the redeeming presence of Christ in the world."[31] The Eucharist is therefore more than a celebration. It is a call to action for every baptized Christian. Eucharist and baptism, taken together, are the Christian call to discipleship and action that Jesus united into one when he asks each one of us: "Are you able to drink the cup that I drink, or be baptized with the baptism that I am baptized with?" (Mk 10:38)

Baptism and Eucharist as a Challenge to Ministry

Baptism is a challenge to ministry because it relates us to our Christian mission to serve the reign of God. If we accept our baptism, dying, and rising with Jesus Christ, then there are consequences and responsibilities. Baptism means that, with Jesus, we must love unto death. Jesus' willingness to suffer and die in order to provide a new life for his friends is the saving sacrament of God's life-giving love for us. To share this willingness to love others with Jesus is the heart of Christian discipleship and ministry.

Baptism also means that we share in the joy of Jesus' resurrection. Jesus is a continuing reality. He is risen, and will always be so. He has not "gone back" on this in any way whatsoever. He is with us, and we are meant to identify with and proclaim this experience of the Risen Lord here and now. To proclaim only Jesus' suffering, and point out that we, too, must therefore suffer, is to proclaim only half of the story. Paul reminds us that, in our baptism into Jesus, we now share the mind of Christ. We now have a "Christ consciousness." This fact is marked by the sign of the cross on the forehead as part of the baptismal rite. In baptism, we also share in the Spirit of Jesus, the source of our new life. Thus, the mystery of baptism is not a hiddenness, but a revelation. It is the revelation that we are brought, in a very intimate way, into the love and life of the triune God, in Jesus Christ, and in the Holy Spirit. We are drawn into the solidarity of the community of the Trinity.

In baptism, we are given a new identity. We are defined as sons and daughters, and partners, of the triune God, and as God wants to live in solidarity with us, so we are called to do the same for others. When we are baptized into the life, death, and resurrection of Jesus, we are baptized with him into solidarity for all humanity. Migliore highlights this solidarity when he states:

> Baptism creates a solidarity that defies and shatters the divisions and barriers that sinful human beings have created. Racism, sexism, and other ideologies of separation are doubly reprehensible when they exist within or are supported by the Christian church, since they are a denial of the solidarity which is God's intention for human life made in the image and reconciled by the activity of the triune God.[32]

This solidarity extends to all of creation. We cannot remain indifferent to the exploitation and destruction of all forms of life on earth, and to the constant depletion of the earth's resources. God's promise of salvation, and the fullness of the coming reign of God, includes the transformation of everything that God has created.

When we are baptized, we enter into solidarity with the community of the faithful, and when we participate in the Eucharist, we are challenged to share this communion of solidarity with others, and with all of creation. In baptism and Eucharist, we Christians receive our identity as disciples, and our vocation to be active in the world. Through the sacraments,

God's grace strengthens us for our mission and our vocation, and we share in the mission and vocation of Jesus. To be a Christian is to be a disciple, joining with Jesus in his work of bringing about the reign of God. Sharing in Jesus' mission, through baptism, means accepting the responsibility to do something in order to achieve this mission. Knowing about it is not enough. There can be no such thing as an "inactive" disciple. What Jesus began was meant to be carried out by subsequent generations of disciples. Each Christian community has to decide how this is to be done, depending on the context in which one lives, and on the most urgent needs of the community. Christian commitment is very particular and unfolds, not in the abstract, but in the actual situations in which it finds itself. We cannot heal and liberate in general; we heal and liberate the people we come in contact with.

If a person accepts the challenge of his or her mission as a member of a Christian community, then that person's own life goals will be integrated into that mission. The goals of the reign of God will be their personal goals, too. It is the decision to live for Jesus Christ, to be one of his disciples. Once again, the community has a responsibility. New members initiated into a faith community will accept this mission only if the community itself is actively involved. If a community is not really committed to its goal, then new members cannot become part of fulfilling that mission, and individuals will be unable to acquire a sense of sharing the mission of Jesus Christ. If, however, the community lives the sharing graces of the Eucharist, then the solidarity of each member's baptism will be evident.

The Eucharist is the sharing of the divine life with humanity. In the life, death, and resurrection of Jesus, God shares everything with us. We participate in this sharing when we, in turn, share our lives with others. At the table of the Eucharist no one is left hungry. We eat and drink the abundance of our God. The Eucharist is about hospitality; all are welcome. In the deepest meaning of symbol, it is the reality of the welcoming of the reign of God. Jesus shared his meals with the marginalized and the outcasts; so, too, must we. If it is the chief way in which the church exhibits its sacramentality, then the Eucharist must be a place in the church's life where salvation for all is effectively symbolized, proclaimed, and practised. Our Eucharists and our church communities are impoverished if they do not witness to the fact that Jesus has redeemed all peoples and welcomes them as friends.[33]

Jesus puts the same question to each of us that he put to his disciples as he called them to a life of conversion, service, and loving communion. We are all called to be God's people, to join with Jesus in a life of service in the foundation of a new community, and to accept the invitation of the Holy Spirit, who sends us out into the world to witness as his disciples. As a community of disciples, we are called to proclaim the gospel and to be witnesses to the reign of God. How this calling of the whole People of God is structured must meet the needs of both the local and the wider community. It must also allow each member to use, for the greater glory of God, and for God's people, the gifts with which God has endowed them. A community's refusal to recognize and use each person's gifts, and consequently its inability to provide for the needs of the community, is a communal sin. It is a refusal to recognize the fullness of discipleship to which each baptized person is called, and it does not build up the community of love that we celebrate in the Eucharist. The Holy Spirit gives diverse gifts that can enrich the life of the community. If these are to be fully effective, then the community must publicly endorse and mandate certain of these charisms. New challenges and new needs call for new mandates and a recognition of new ministries. The ordained ministers and the whole community need to be attentive and prepared to respond to this challenge: Are we able to live the baptism with which Jesus was baptized? Are we able to offer the cup that he offered? Are we able to do so in memory of him?

Chapter 6

Ecclesiology:
The Church as Trinitarian Community

"For where two or three are gathered in my name, I am there among them." (Mt 18:20)

Introduction

Ecclesiology is the theological study of the church. The church is an aspect of Christian existence, and the doctrine of the church has been an essential part of Christian faith since its earliest beginnings. The Apostles' Creed contains the statement of belief in "the holy catholic church," which is expanded in the Nicene Creed as "the one, holy, catholic, and apostolic church."[1] Belief in the church, together with the initial faith in God as Trinity, are constitutive affirmations for all believers. Just as the nature of the Trinity is not an abstract teaching about God apart from human experience, ecclesiology is not the study of an abstract understanding of the church, but the account of a people who gather in common faith and common mission.

The fundamental nature of the church is rooted in the nature of revelation. The church stems from the essence of Christianity itself: the self-communication of God to humanity in Jesus Christ. There is a connection between God, Jesus Christ, and humanity on the one hand, and the church on the other. The nature of the church depends upon the relationship between these three, and they come together in the concrete reality of what the church is:

the whole body of persons who are called by God the Father to acknowledge the Lordship of Jesus, the Son, in word and sacrament, in witness and service, and, through the power of the Holy Spirit, to collaborate with Jesus' historic mission for the sake of the kingdom of God.[2]

This communal dimension of the church as a whole body, or community of persons, underscores its inherent social structure. As we have observed, the relational nature of God and humanity means that the social dimension is integral to the essence of religious expression and living. The doctrine of the church is based upon this essential element of human life. Our communal witness as church links revelation and human experience in a way that is decisive for how we live our faith. This gives rise to some of the most far-reaching questions concerning theological anthropology and a theology for ministry. Our life as a community of faith reveals our understanding of ministry and Christian mission. As a visible church community we see how authentically we live out our faith, and how pastoral needs can challenge our practice of faith if it does not reflect the loving action of our triune God manifested in the teaching and example of Jesus Christ. The Christian doctrine of the church and its praxis are of major importance for all who are engaged in church service, and for anyone proposing to engage in pastoral ministry of any kind.

I: Welcome the Poor, the Marginalized, and the Outcasts

The disciples who followed Jesus were given a mission: preach the good news of liberation and love to all peoples, but especially to the poor, the marginalized, the outcasts, and sinners. Welcome them into a community, in which the first will be last, and those who want to be first will be asked to serve others. Jesus modelled this mission in his own life and ministry. When he washed his disciples' feet, he directed that, to serve in his kingdom, they must do the same for others, and they must also be humble enough to allow others to wash their feet and to serve them. Jesus wanted his community to be identified by these characteristics of welcoming, service, and humility. The roots of the contemporary church are to welcome and serve one another in the name of Jesus Christ.

The foundation of the church is found in Jesus' preaching to the people of Israel. He wanted to call them into God's *basileia*. *Basileia* is a Greek translation of the Aramaic word that means "God's rule," or "reign of God." The *basileia* of God is the substance of Jesus' message. In Jesus, and in his works, the *basileia* is at hand (Mk 1:15), and with it the salvation of humanity. The *basileia* is open to everyone, but, above all, to the marginalized. The fullness of the *basileia* will be in the future, as Jesus makes clear when he asks his disciples to pray for the coming of the *basileia* in the Lord's Prayer (Mt 6:10). We have yet to inherit the *basileia*, which only God can bring about. Paul distinguishes between the *basileia* of Christ, which is the church, and the *basileia* of God, which Jesus preached: God "has rescued us from the power of darkness and transferred us into the kingdom of his beloved Son, in whom we have redemption, the forgiveness of sins" (Col 1:13). The *basileia* cannot therefore be related directly to the church. Michael Fahey points out:

> The community that emerged from Jesus' preaching, life, death, and resurrection, the church, cannot be identified purely and simply with God's reign (*basileia*). The church is, rather, a privileged locus for the advancement of the rule of God still to be realized. Some modern catholic writers describe the church as an instrument of God's reign. This formulation is potentially misleading if it suggests that God's reign comes about through our efforts, when clearly it occurs by God's gracious and free intervention.... The kingdom of God does not depend on our actions but is God's promised eschatological work.[3]

After Jesus' preaching on the *basileia* was rejected by a large proportion of Israel, he changed the vision of his mission. He then not only preached to the "holy remnant," but began to initiate his disciples into the deeper mysteries of his mission and his impending death. He knew that there would be some time between his death and the realization of the *basileia*. Jesus trained his disciples as teachers and preachers so that his message and mission would be passed on. This hope is especially evident when he instructed them to "do this in memory of me" as a community of believers at the Last Supper.

The New Testament writers were trying to live as the community of faith in the Risen Lord. There was never a "churchless" period in the New Testament after the resurrection. This is clear when, after Peter's declaration of faith, Jesus promised: "You are Peter, and on this rock I will build my church, and the gates of Hades will not prevail against it" (Mt 16:18). Jesus also promises the Holy Spirit, who will empower and inspire this community of believers. The relationship with the Spirit of God is an important link between Jesus and the early church.

What is the Church?

The word "church" is based on the Greek word *ekklesia*. An *ekklesia* was a legislative assembly of people to which only free citizens with full rights could belong. The original Greek term had no religious significance whatsoever, but refers both to the dignity of the people gathered and to the legality of the assembly itself. The Greek translation of the Bible (the *Septuagint*) used *ekklesia* to interpret the Hebrew word *qahal,* which, together with the term *edah,* expresses the religious assembly of the Israelites.[4] The early Christian community did not understand itself as distinct from Judaism, and they simply used the Hebrew term to refer to their own gatherings of prayer. In this context, *ekklesia* was understood as the holy people assembled for worship. "Church" meant the Lord's congregation. Therefore, while the Christian community took its name from the Greek assembly, its meaning derives from the original Hebrew for a people gathered to praise God, rather than from the Greek translation. The church is obviously not simply a legal gathering, but a people gathered for, and in the name of, God.

When Gentiles were admitted to the community the distinction between the church and Judaism became evident. Shortly thereafter, *ekklesia* was applied only to the Christian community. The New Testament use of the term, and especially Paul's use of *ekklesia*, confirms this understanding of church as an assembled community. In reference to the specifically Christian assembly, it is the new community of believers who gather, through the power of the Holy Spirit, to praise God in response to the ministry, death, and resurrection of Jesus Christ. The nature of this community is continually qualified by the one who summons it. The *ekklesia* belongs to God because God has called it into being, dwells within it, and rules over it (Acts 20:28; 1 Cor 1:2). In some instances it is also qualified by the phrase "the church of Christ" (Rom 16:16; Gal 1:22), and by the joint phrase "the church...in God the Father, and the Lord Jesus Christ" (1 Thess 1:1; 2 Thess 1:1).[5]

Gathered in the name of the triune God, *ekklesia* refers to a people who have been transformed to a new way of being human in relationship to God and with others. It identifies a community characterized by love, mutuality, interdependence, forgiveness, and service. Ecclesial life is the enacted new community of free persons, which is centred on God's love in Jesus Christ, and empowered by the Holy Spirit. *Ekklesia* highlights the impossibility of an individualistic Christianity. The life of love of Jesus Christ and the Trinity can only take place in interpersonal relationships, and can only be found in *ekklesia*. The community is necessarily united: all of the New Testament authors write as members of the one church. There is no fragmentation among them. They are all built on the foundation of the Apostles, and all have Jesus as their centre.[6]

Church unity derives from the understanding that *ekklesia* is the church of God. In most cases *ekklesia* refers to a local church, but it is also understood in a plural form. Paul is the first to use the term "churches." In Paul's writings, *ekklesia* refers both to a single local church, and also to the wider church. While *ekklesia* refers to a community of believers gathered in a specific area—for example, the church at Corinth—it is also understood as constituted prior to and apart from such local assemblies. *Ekklesia*, in the sense of the wider church, does not refer simply to Christian churches dispersed throughout the world, or to the totality of local churches. It is the universal church as a mystical, eschatological entity, in line with Jesus' understanding of *basileia*. The universal church is the heavenly church gathered around the Risen Christ in anticipation of its final consummation. This has profound implications for each church community that gathers in the local community. Miroslav Volf explains:

> The alleged relation of actualizations between universal and local church as well as the notion of the identity of the two is grounded theologically in a certain understanding of the relation between Christ and Church…. Just as Christ is present in every local church, and acts within it, so also the universal church which together with Christ as a mystical person, is present in every local church, acting within or identical with it.[7]

The local church is not a subdivision of the universal church, nor is the universal church the sum total of local churches. For example, there is no Corinthian dimension of the church, but "the church of God that is in Corinth" (1 Cor 1:2). God is present and acts within each local church. Each local church is complete.

Images of the Church in the New Testament

Church is not an abstract concept; it is about people and their relationship with God. Two major images of the church in the New Testament capture this reality of our relationship to God and how it affects our community life: the church as "the People of God," and the church as "the Body of Christ."

The "People of God" originally identified the natural and religious unity of Israel and the covenant that God established with it. In Hebrew thought, people formed a whole, a corporate personality, and each human person derived meaning and importance insofar as the individual was part of this corporate reality. Israel fashioned its corporate reality as the "People of God." The Hebrew people believed that God had called them into the fidelity of the covenant.

In the New Testament, "People of God" expresses the eschatological consciousness of the church, and this established the continuity of the church with the People of God of the covenant community. This was an explicit recognition of the solidarity between the church and Israel. The church was identified as the Israel of God (Gal 6:16), and God was known as the God of Israel (Mt 2:6; Lk 1:54, 68). Gentiles were incorporated into the People of Israel (Rom 11:11-12), and they also inherited the hope of Israel (Acts 28:20). There were, of course, those who naturally inherited this hope because of biological descent or cultural identity, but what constituted the People of God was the communal relationship to God that was the result of God's promise. The community of the People of God included all who had lived by faith in God's covenant promises (Mt 8:11; Lk 13:28-30; Heb 11).[8]

Lumen Gentium reiterates the image of the church as the People of God. The Council drew upon this biblical image to emphasize the human and communal nature of the church, rather than its institutional and hierarchical aspects. The Council also stressed that everything that is said about the People of God applies to the total community of the church, pastors as well as other faithful; it does not refer to the laity alone. We are all one people:

> "Behold the days shall come, saith the Lord, and I will make a
> new covenant with the House of Israel, and with the house of

Judah.... I will give my law in their bowels, and I will write it in their heart, and I will be their God, and they shall be my people.... For all shall know me, from the least of them even to the greatest, saith the Lord." (Jer 31:31-34) Christ instituted this new covenant, that is to say, the new testament, in his blood. (cf. 1 Cor 11:25), by calling together a people made up of Jew and Gentile, making them one, not according to the flesh, but in the Spirit. This was to be the new people of God. (*LG* 9)[9]

The image of the People of God on its own, however, cannot express the whole reality of the church. The new People of God gather in the name of Jesus Christ and in the power of the Holy Spirit; therefore, a christological and pneumatological dimension is constitutive of any image of the church. From an image presented by Paul (1 Cor 6:15; Eph 1:22-23; Col 1:24), and in continuity with tradition (St. Clement of Rome, Origen, St. Augustine), the church is also referred to as the "Body of Christ." The image of the Body of Christ identifies the church intimately with Jesus Christ, and provides a solid foundation for the communal relationships of its members with one another. This image is grounded in the union of each Christian and the risen body of Jesus. When Christians share in the bread of the Eucharist, they become one body with Christ. This is especially evident in Pauline ecclesiology: "Because there is one bread, we who are many are one body, for we all partake of the one bread" (1 Cor 10:17). The one body of Jesus Christ has reconciled us to God by his death (Eph 2:16-17; Col 1:18). The church has also become the one body where the Holy Spirit dwells, and Christians themselves are called one body (Col 3:15).

The image also refers to the many members and their ministries. It relates to the many charisms and offices of the church; their multiplicity and variety does not compromise the fundamental unity of the Body of Christ, because the Body of Christ binds Christians together as *koinonia*. The church is the communion of life that has Jesus Christ as its centre, and through which a new humanity in the Spirit of Christ emerges. The reality of this communal life is expressed in many ways, but they all point to the interrelationships between humanity and God, and members with one another. The members of Christ's body are in him, and he is in them. (Gal 2:20); they are baptized into him (1 Cor 12:13); the Holy Spirit is present in the church community (Rom 8:9-11; 1 Cor 6:19; 12:4-11), and all its members are knit together by the power of the love of the triune God. All the trinitarian elements of *perichoresis*, interpenetration and interdependence, are brought together in the description of the church as the Body of Christ.

All believers are equal members of the Body of Christ. In the church, each person is a member of the same body; each is bound in an intimate and significant way to Jesus Christ. Each individual body has become a member of Christ's body, and this should determine what they do with it: "We, who are many, are one body in Christ, and individually we are members of one another" (Rom 12:5). This requires that all recognize their mutual dependence. Each member, no matter what their role, shares in the common glory and life of the Body of Christ, and each, no matter how prominent their gift, must always remember in humility that they have received this gift from Jesus Christ for the sake of the whole body: "For by the grace given to me I say to everyone among you not to think of yourself more highly than you ought to think, but to think with sober judgment, each according to the measure of faith that God has assigned" (Rom 12:3). All the spiritual gifts of the church are mediated through the Body of Christ to its members, and through its members to the Body. The same truth applies to the various types of ministries, and to the various races and classes, which, in Jesus Christ, are reconciled to one another. There are many members, but there can only be one Body, Jesus Christ.[10]

These major images of the church as the People of God and as the mystical Body of Christ emphasize the church's dependence on the triune God and recall the interdependence of all of its members, past, present, and future. The life of the church is a life of communion as the People of God, in Jesus Christ, and in the power of the Holy Spirit.

Church as the Perichoretic Image of the Triune God

The organization of the church is called to reflect the image of the triune God, and ecclesiology is in close relationship to trinitarian doctrine: "the church shares faith as a people brought into the unity of the Father, the Son, and the Holy Spirit," (*LG* 4) and an understanding of the church's mission and ministry is grounded in this same image. The church community flows from the perichoretic life of the Trinity: trinitarian communion expresses the love and life that constitute the nature of God. A trinitarian ecclesiology is based on the fundamental affirmation that the God who is revealed in Jesus Christ, through the continuing activity of the Holy Spirit, is a God of extravagant love. Further, according to trinitarian doctrine, the nature of God is relational and communal, and humanity is called to live this communion with God, and with one another. The church is the community that is called into being and sent into the world to serve in the name of, and in the power of, this same triune God. The church lives its mission and ministry to the fullest when it corresponds to this trinitarian communion. This is not to propose a blueprint for church structure; rather, it is to provide principles and values that should characterize and underlie church governance and practice. La Cugna notes:

> The trinitarian doctrine of God, as the basis for a trinitarian ecclesiology, might not specify the exact form of structure and community appropriate to the church, but it does provide the critical principle against which we can measure present institutional arrangements. Very simply, we may ask whether our institution, rituals, and administrative practices foster elitism, discrimination, competition, or any of the several 'archisms,' or whether the church is run like God's household: a domain of inclusiveness, interdependence, and cooperation, structured according to the model of 'perichoresis' among persons.[11]

The perichoretic relationship of the Trinity further emphasizes the mutuality of communion: the result of communion is community. In the New Testament, it refers to communion with God, with the Son, with the Holy Spirit, and also to the communion among believers. There are two dimensions to this communion, a vertical dimension representing our contact with God, and a horizontal dimension representing our bond with other Christians. The union of persons with God, and with one another, is accomplished by the grace and the power of the Holy Spirit. It is part of Jesus' prayer for his disciples: "I ask not only on behalf of these, but also on behalf of those who will believe in me through their word, that they may all be one" (Jn 17:20). Every person, as a bearer of the Spirit, participates in constituting this unity, and together they constitute the mission of the church. *Gaudium et Spes* states:

> By virtue of her mission to shed on the whole world the radiance of the Gospel message, and to unify under one Spirit all [people] of whatever nation, race, or culture, the church stands forth as a

sign of that [companionship] which allows honest dialogue and invigorates it.

Such a mission requires in the first place that we foster within the church herself mutual esteem, reverence and harmony through full recognition of lawful diversity. Thus all those who compose the one People of God, both pastors and the general faithful, can engage in dialogue with ever-abounding fruitfulness. For the bonds which unite the faithful are mightier than anything which divides them. Hence, let there be unity in what is necessary, freedom in what is unsettled, and charity in any case. (*GS* 92)

The constant renewal of the presence of the Father, the Son, and the Spirit in the People of God is the source of the church's fidelity to its mission of constant renewal. If the inner life of the church is the image of the inner life of the triune God, then the mission of the church is also the same as that of the Trinity: Perichoretic communion is constitutive of the nature of the church, its mission, and its ministry. While the church is far from reaching the fullness of this communion, as exemplified in the mission and ministry of Jesus, the vocation of all its members remains: to serve others and to promote the reign of God. The mission of every Christian is the same as the mission of Jesus: to do the will and work of God, and to proclaim the good news of salvation and liberation: "the obligation of spreading the faith is imposed on every disciple of Christ, according to his or her ability." (*LG* 17)

Church Mission and Ministry Today

Discipleship in the New Testament church differs from discipleship in the church today. While the early church did not have the same church structure as we have presently, there was a structure that shaped the mission and ministry of the early community based on its understanding of its call to proclaim the Word of God. While there were some members who served in a leadership capacity, the whole congregation was involved in the decision-making process. Local churches were guided by presbyters, and some members were appointed by the community as overseers. "Overseer" was the original meaning of the word "bishop," or *episkopos*. There was no radical distinction between the so-called charismatic ministries and the administrative ministries. All were considered as the gifts of the Holy Spirit. Some had a specifically charismatic character, for example, the gift of tongues, and others were clearly administrative or institutional, such as teaching and presiding. Whatever the ministry, they were all for the sake of service to the community, and never for the sake of domination. Jesus is the model for all ministry whose example was to give his life for others: "For the Son of Man came not to be served but to serve, and to give his life as a ransom for many" (Mk 10:45).[12]

Unlike the early Christian community, there *is* a radical distinction between church ministries today. Most members would agree that the church subsists through the participation of all its members, is constituted through them by the Holy Spirit, and that both the laity and the officeholders contribute to its continuation and renewal. What is disputed is *how* this occurs. Yet it must occur because all members of the church are stewards of God's grace in their words and in their actions, commensurate with their calling, and as endowed with the gift of God's Spirit. All are empowered by the same Spirit to contribute to the worship and the entire life of the church. The church lives and flourishes only to the extent that its good news of liberation is mediated through a mutuality of service manifest in the variety of gifts of the Spirit that is given to each of its members.

The presence of Christ that constitutes the church is mediated not simply through the ordained ministry, but through the whole assembly of the People of God, the Body of Christ. The whole congregation functions as church to all of God's children brought into being by the power of the Holy Spirit. Consequently, every member of the congregation is called to engage in ministry, and to make decisions about church leadership. The church is a community of free and equal persons, and as communal beings living in *koinonia,* it is the community based on the non-hierarchical doctrine of the Trinity. This understanding of the whole people of God as bearers of the Word of God, in the action of ministry, has been part of our language about church for several decades now, but it has remained at a somewhat theoretical level. Individual, non-ordained members of the church still have a deep-seated difficulty in accepting their sacred responsibility. This is not because they are unwilling or incapable, but because they are usually not encouraged to see themselves as having a distinctive charism that can manifest itself in church ministry.

There has been an enormous shift in how the term "ministry" is understood since Vatican II. Before this time, ministry was the work of ordained clergy; not even the services provided by vowed men and women in religious orders were called ministry. It was not until certain functions that were previously performed only by priests—such as distributing the Eucharist—were opened up to others that the term was expanded to include church services provided by the non-ordained. Today, "ministry" applies to any service that a person provides in the name of, and as an expression of, the Christian community. Grounded in the gifts of the grace of the Holy Spirit, ministry in the life and experience of the church is a much larger reality than the ministry of the ordained clergy. It consists of a broad spectrum of services that have come into existence over the centuries, and that continues to expand. New forms of service for nourishment and leadership in the church continue to emerge, under the guidance of the Holy Spirit, as the needs of our church community grow and as new challenges in the world demand new ways of providing service to those who need to hear the liberating news of the gospel.

Vatican II treated issues concerning church ministries in a number of its documents. The Constitution on the Sacred Liturgy (*Sacrosanctum Concilium*)[13] emphasized that the entire congregation—that is, the presiding minister and the gathered assembly—is the agent of the church's liturgical life. It declared that all members of the worshipping community take an active part in liturgical celebrations, in gathering, prayer, and song, and it outlined the rules for all members in the proper performance of the prayer life of the church. A major result was the expansion of the forms of ministry exercised in the celebration of the Eucharist. Ministries such as acolyte, lector, distributors of communion, and the bringing of communion to those unable to attend the parish eucharistic celebration were opened up to the non-ordained. *Sacrosanctum Concilium* reminded the church, and fully recognized, that the entire church as the People of God shares Jesus' prophetic, priestly, and royal ministry.[14]

The Council also included decrees on bishops' pastoral office in the church, on priestly formation, on the renewal of religious life, and on the Apostolate of the Laity (*Apostolicam Actuositatem*).[15] In the decrees on bishops and priests, the Council reiterated much of the traditional understandings of these offices' function, but in its decree on the laity, the role of the laity was brought to the fore: "Although a 'lay apostolate' has existed in the church since the days of our Lord in Jerusalem, it was not until the Second Vatican Council that the church's official thinking on the matter was stated in a conciliar decree."[16] The decree states:

> The laity derive the right and duty with respect to the apostolate from their union with Christ their Head. Incorporated into Christ's mystical Body through baptism and strengthened by the power of the Holy Spirit through confirmation, they are assigned to the apostolate by the Lord himself. They are consecrated into a royal priesthood, and a holy people (cf. 1 Pt 2:4-10) in order that they may offer spiritual sacrifices through everything they do, and may witness to Christ throughout the world. (*AA* 3)

The decree describes the nature, character, and diversity of the lay apostolate, states its basic principles, and gives pastoral directives for its more effective exercise (*AA* 1). The decree clearly explains the vision of the servant-church, a church created and formed for ministry and enlivened by its ministries. It ends by exhorting the laity to listen attentively to the voice of Jesus Christ:

> Once again he sends them into every town and place where he himself will come. (Lk 10:1) Thus they can show that they are His co-workers in the various forms and methods of the church's own apostolate, which must be constantly adapted to the new needs of the times. May they also abound in the works of God, knowing that they will not labour in vain when their labour is for him. (*AA* 33)

The "new needs of the times" for us in today's church bring us to the new reality of a group of women and men who are now serving the faith community in a way that is quite different from the broader understanding of the apostolate of the laity.

We Are All Equal and Interdependent

Since all the members of the church are equal and interdependent, then the life of the church, if it is to reflect the communion of the triune God, must actively witness to this equality and mutuality. This can be done most effectively when the charismata of servant leadership of office are integrated into this mutuality. This was the case in the early community, when there was no radical distinction between charismatic and administrative ministries because all came from the same Spirit of Christ. There is such a radical distinction in these ministries today that another approach to the question is required. Volf suggests making a distinction between the office and the spirituality of the ministry involved. He explains this in more depth when he says:

> Officeholders do not stand opposite the church as those acting exclusively in *persona christi*. Since the Spirit of Christ acts in them not by the power of their office, but rather in the execution of their ministry, their actions do not differ in principle from those of any other member of the church. Insofar as each person contributes in his or her own specific way to the various aspects of church life, that person is acting as a 'representative' of Christ to those affected by that action. This does not eliminate the inevitable polarity between ministry in *persona christi* and the congregation, but it does decentralize it, and in so doing, overcome the bipolarity between 'office holders' and 'congregation.' Spiritual activity and receptivity are no longer assigned to two different groups of persons; that is, every person acts in *persona christi* and every person receives this activity.[17]

Fundamentally, we are one in Christ. Distinctions of office and charismata are necessary, but secondary and provisional. No personal power is attained by either of them: they are a loving service, a sacred responsibility. The real distinction is only evidenced in a greater love of God, and for one another.

Obviously, not everyone participates in the same way, or with the same degree of intensity, but while there is no doubt that the officeholders in the church have an indispensable role, the life of the church is not ordered around them. The Holy Spirit does not constitute the church exclusively through its officeholders, but, rather, through the person and gifts of every member who serves in the community.[18] Offices represent a particular type of charism. Similar to all other ministries in the church, the ministry of the ordained officeholders is based on our common baptism, together with the specific charismata bestowed upon officeholders. All who serve the church community in a specifically mandated way also have the grace of the charismata of their specific ministry; there can be no difference in principle between officeholders and other members of the church. The distinction between the general priesthood of all believers and the particular priesthood does not divide the church into two groups. There are not two priesthoods, one having only the general characteristic, priesthood, and one having both the general and the particular. The distinction refers to two dimensions in the service of every member of the church. All Christians, on the basis of common baptism, have become priests, and, on the basis of their respective charismata, all realize their priesthood in their own way. All members of the church, both officeholders and lay persons, are fundamentally equal.

Such equality, and such equitable distinction of charismata, calls for common responsibility for the life of the church. The common responsibility that is implied here is not one that would see official church leadership usurped. On the contrary, common responsibility is compatible with the charismata of church leadership, but in the context of the equal distribution and understanding of charismata, it obtains a different profile. It is impossible for leaders, whether ordained or not, to do everything in the church by themselves. Good leadership animates all members of the community, engages their charismata for service and ministry, and co-ordinates all of these activities. Leaders are also responsible for the nurturing of a mature church community, that is, a group of people who have reached, or are striving toward, a level of authenticity with themselves, with God, and with one another. It is also realizing that, while all the members of the church community have charismata, no one member, or any group of members, has all charismata. The fullness of the gifts of the Holy Spirit are to be found in the entirety of the local church.

The Call for a Broadened Understanding of Church Ministry and Leadership

In the Good Friday general intercessions we pray not only for the pope, bishops, priests, and deacons, but "for all who hold a ministry in the church."[19] The faith community recognizes that, alongside the ministerial offices of bishop, priest, and deacon, there are other ministries that are identical neither with these nor with the responsibilities that fall to a Christian who is simply a member of the church community. Apart from these three classic offices in the church, other ministries, in analogous fashion, "actually share in the mission and task of sacred office in the church as ultimately one single office."[20] A person whose profession, in all its aspects, serves the church, and permeates all of his or her life, shares in the official mission of the church in relation to the people that he or she serves. One could say that such ministries, in some way, participate in the sacramentality of these classic offices. This statement would not mitigate against the priestly orders, since there are differentiations within them in any case.

New needs and challenges in the church are calling for a broadening of our understanding of ministry and how it is mandated in the church. The fact that the number of men and women entering the ordained priesthood and religious orders has declined significantly has brought about a crisis in many of the forms of ministry that have been traditionally exercised by clergy and religious, especially in parishes, schools, and hospitals. In a few cases there has been an increase in the number of lay people serving in these ministries. The downside of this crisis is that some parishes have ceased to be able to celebrate the Eucharist regularly, and thus fail in Jesus' command to "Do this in memory of me." Some parishes have to rely on communion services instead, or on the occasional presence of an ordained priest for Eucharist, reconciliation, and marriages. Despite the crisis, and its inability to serve the People of God, the official church refuses to open these ministries to all lay people, in order to mandate them to assume full pastoral sacramental participation in the life of the church. Meanwhile, the crisis intensifies, and more and more people find themselves in communities that cannot meet their sacramental and pastoral needs. It leaves one wondering just what criteria are used in deciding who should and who should not minister in the service of God's people.

Above all, the response of every heart to God's task for each person is at issue. The task varies in its form, but not in its fundamental context: the call to be sons and daughters of God in Jesus Christ. "There are varieties of gifts, but the same Spirit; and there are varieties of service, but the same Lord; and there are varieties of activities, but it is the same God who activates all of them in everyone" (1 Cor 12:4-6). The ministries that the People of God have exercised for each other throughout the history of the church show a rich variety of service. Faith in the church involves a continued trust that the Holy Spirit will continue to empower the members of the church community to meet the needs of the church as it lives out its mission to serve the faithful from one generation to the next. Our faith in the church also means that we trust the church will always witness to the mystery of Christ that constitutes it, in continuous service to those who need to hear the good news of Jesus' liberation. By opening ourselves to the power of the diversity of the Spirit, we will be able to continue Jesus' mission. The same God, the same Lord, the same Spirit of the triune God is still at work in the People of God, serving the church through the abundant variety of gifts given to each of its members for the building of the Body of Christ.

II: A De-institutionalized Church

The corollary to a church leadership responsible for nurturing a mature church is the additional responsibility of all members of the church to strive toward a spiritual maturity in regard to themselves, God, and other members. This does not seem to be happening in the present official church structure, yet, unless it does, we cannot have the broadened understanding of ministry that is necessary for the full participation of all its members that is necessary to serve the growing needs of the church. If the church is not structured as a community, then we cannot possibly live the communion of the life of the triune God that can make this a reality.

This trinitarian principle of communion opens up the question of community and institution: that is, how people actually structure their common life. This brings us to the heart of the matter: Does the church function as a community, or as an institution? Does it function as both? Does this raise once again the question of the local and universal church? Can the church serve in the name of Jesus Christ by existing as an institution, or can we only witness to, and teach, the inner peace and freedom of Jesus through community? Many, if not most, people today would say that the official church is synonymous with the institutional church. Yet one major difference between a community structure and an institutional structure is that communities foster relationships while institutions impose a series of self-alienating roles. There is no opportunity for loving relationships within the structures of institutions, and where there are no loving relationships there is no opportunity to imitate the triune God. A simple illustration can help to highlight the difference.

Institution	Community
The person is usually nameless as far as officeholders are concerned	The person is named and known, and called forth
The person plays a subscribed role, divorced from his or her true self	The person lives out his or her authentic self
The person is needed for the tasks that he or she fulfills, and is seen as dispensable	The person is nourished and loved for the gifts that he or she contributes to the community, and is seen as irreplaceable and unique

Only a de-institutionalized church can work for the good of all God's people. No one is denying the necessity of the bureaucratic offices of institutional structures, but they do have inherent limitations. Institutions have a limited ability to serve people's needs fully, and they must not promise what they cannot deliver: human dignity and freedom. There is limited value to institutional structures as far as the human person is concerned. This is why people often feel marginalized in the church. They need community, but they are offered institution. Communities know a person's name, welcome them, and serve them. Institutions, on the other hand, know their statistics. A church that operates as an institution establishes priorities and shapes pastoral strategies that ignore people's needs, and as Fahey cautions, "whoever neglects the insights of the poor, the oppressed, or the victimized does so at the peril of formulating an impoverished ecclesiology."[21]

It is our shared responsibility and personal task to understand the role institutions play in our lives, and to develop a critical attitude toward them. When we have come to such an understanding, perhaps we will realize that we have to de-institutionalize ourselves. How we do this will vary for each individual, but if we regard ourselves as spiritually mature, then we must have reached some kind of critical conclusions about the validity made by contemporary society and its institutional structures with regard to the meaning of our existence.[22] In many respects, institutional structures fall short. They cannot, for example, nurture love or happiness, which happens only in community relationships, yet the dynamic between the individual and the institution claims a connection to humanity and human happiness, and ultimately deals with the broader issues of that which brings meaning to our life.

One way of approaching this issue is to start with our own consciousness in relation to the institutional structures we belong to—family, school, church, government. How do they operate? What attaches us to these institutions? Do we see them as they really are? Unfortunately, the moment we encounter a situation, we bring our own preconceived notions about how we think we should behave in relation to that situation. We play a role, and put our ego at the centre. We want our ego to be satisfied; this is the source of many of our problems. What is needed is a transformation, a conversion, a liberation of our consciousness. This is not an evolutionary or automatic process, however, and the quest for full personal realization is a constant. Merton calls it "the secret of liberation." The process of Christian conversion requires each person to be able to stand on his or her own two feet. The essence of being of every person, as created in the image of God, is becoming: one strives continuously to become one's full, authentic, and real self, one's Godself. It is a maturation process in which the person participates more fully in his or her own development. More and more today, people are becoming the creators of their own milieu. If such freedom is constitutive of human nature, then it is no less true that responsible freedom in its members is the essence of church. Such conversion is radical. It means that we have to look at things from a different perspective because we have been turned around. It means that we are called to greater personal and communal authenticity.

When we consider the institutions in which we move and have our life today, however, how many of us feel and act as persons of spiritual freedom? One way to explore this question is to consider the categories of dependence, independence, codependence, and interdependence. At some time in their lives, all people are necessarily dependent on a variety of institutional structures, but as they mature, they grow in independence and carve a space for who they are as individuals within the dynamic of interpersonal and communal relationships. When seeking such independence, one of two things can happen, however. They can either become so independent that they become isolated individuals, inept at healthy interpersonal and communal relationships, or they can become codependent on other individuals and institutions. In either case, they are not free to act as authentic, converted persons, living a life for self, God, and others. They essentially become trapped in their own ego. To achieve a level of personal freedom means to work through these dependencies, because total inner transformation and liberation cannot be nourished in such institutional dependence or isolation. Institutions often inhibit personal freedom. Members are either successfully contained within the institution through some form of coercion, or they rebel and leave. Those who rebel usually take an independent stance, and those who are coerced become immaturely codependent. In either case, some form of maldependency results. The underlying theological, anthropological, and ecclesiological premise is that if we understand Christianity in terms of grace, and the graciousness of a loving God, then we cannot uphold this form of institutional manipulation.

To oppose an institutional structure, to stand over against it, or to challenge it in some way, does not necessarily mean setting up an alternative structure. It is, rather, a question of creating another style of praxis, a different way of translating into reality the idea of the relationship between people and institutional structures. It is also to develop a new way of being an individual in any given institutional structure. To view this new thing, and how it might operate, one can look at the paradigm out of which most of our institutional structures function.

All institutional structures predate us—that is, we are born into them—and there is something worth holding on to in all of them. In our religious structures, we call this "tradition." Our task is to find a way to remain faithful to the Spirit and at the same time call our institutions to the questions that are posed by new situations. This means tapping the deepest roots of our memories and the loftiest creativity of our imagination. Can we, as individuals, redefine our institutions? To take such a step would, for example, call us to a new way of being church. This process is not to be equated with "'consciousness raising,'" although that might be included; it is, rather, an attempt to gain a deeper understanding of who we are as responsible beings, and how we understand ourselves as members of the church.

If we look at the church as the People of God, as the mystical Body of Christ, and as a perichoretic communion, it becomes obvious that *the church was never meant to function as an institution in people's lives.* We must de-institutionalize ourselves, both personally and communally. A sure way to do this is to live in communion with Jesus Christ. To live one's life in such a relationship is the call to conversion and liberation of discipleship. It takes a tremendous amount of understanding, compassion, love, faith, wisdom, patience, and maturity, but it is none other than the call to Christian living and its rewards, rewards that the author of the second letter of Peter talks about in the Christian's call and election:

> His divine power has given us everything needed for life and godliness, through the knowledge of him who called us by his own glory and goodness.... For this very reason, you must make every effort to support your faith with goodness, and goodness with knowledge, and knowledge with self-control, and self-control with endurance, and endurance with godliness, and godliness with mutual affection, and mutual affection with love. For if these things are yours and are increasing among you, they keep you from being ineffective and unfruitful in the knowledge of our Lord Jesus Christ.... Therefore, brothers and sisters, be all the more eager to confirm your call and election, for if you do this, you will never stumble. (2 Pt 1:3-10)

Conversion is a complete freeing of oneself in order to be like Jesus Christ. It is a total state of consciousness that changes one's life completely, and a person involved in this process will find that he or she will be de-institutionalized. It will take one from codependence, or independence, to interdependence. In other words, a person will not allow themselves to be manipulated, coerced, or defined by any institution. Rather than having a maldependency on an institution, they will bring a free, authentic, converted self to its dynamic. Being grounded in such a strong sense of self is crucial to healthy interpersonal relationships. Part of the stress of the human condition—and, in the case of ministry, the all-too-familiar state of burnout—is that the many institutions we belong to demand many different things from us, and each of them defines us in a different way. This can turn us into institutional chameleons, having to change who we are depending on which one we are dealing with at any given time. If we are grounded in our Christian selves as images of God, however, institutions will be less successful in having this negative effect on us. It is the difference between living as a free, personal/relational self, and living an institutional role.

If we allow ourselves to be defined by institutions, rather than reaching a critical maturity toward them, it is more difficult for us to critique them, to stand up against them, or, if necessary, to leave them. Jesus was able to challenge the institutions of his day, such as the family, synagogue, and political structure, because he was so grounded in who he was in himself, in his mission, and before God. Jesus de-institutionalized God when he addressed God as "Abba"; he tells people to leave the dependency of their families, especially their parents, in order to follow him; he broke through the institutional barriers of the synagogue when he cured a bent woman (Lk 13:10-17); and he limited the power of the political structure when he rendered to Caesar what was Caesar's. None of this means that we lack a sense of cultural, social, religious, or political structures. We all belong to them, and we are also in many ways responsible for their continuance. The key issue is that we understand ourselves as freely, and interdependently, working within them, not defined by them. We are God's, and it is God who defines who and what we are.

There is a basic Christian orientation that goes beyond any institutional structure. Paul wrote that there is no longer Jew or Greek, male or female (Gal 3:28), because the Christian must move beyond institutional roles and biases. This orientation points beyond divisions. It respects pluralities, but does not make them ends in themselves. The cumulative result is that the Christian is no longer an individual ego, with prejudices, biases, and dependencies, but one in whom the Spirit of Jesus dwells and has its being: the indwelling of the Holy Spirit in each person. The Christian is open to other people because, essentially, Jesus is present in others. The Christian opens himself or herself to an interdependence and trust that is the result of liberation as created in the image of God. It is a liberty that no one can touch, that no one can effect, that no social, religious, or political circumstance can remove or alter.

In our ministry, it is this liberty that we must strive toward in ourselves, and which we try to bring out in other people. We attempt to free ourselves and others from any institutional bondage that would entrap us. Wherever we have someone nurturing this freedom, we witness the work of the Holy Spirit. Once the fire of the spiritual freedom is lit, it cannot be extinguished. It is the deepest and most essential thing in life: our Godself, our de-institutionalized self.

Church as Freeing Community

It takes a loving, trusting community to develop such freedom in a person, and a person is as free as they are trusting; trusting in themselves, in God, and in others. This type of trust moves us through fear and feelings of inadequacy to love—that is, knowing that we are capable of loving, and that we are lovable. Trust, then, is an integral part of love. It involves the risk of giving more than we receive. It is the gift of oneself in advance, of believing and hoping without any previous reassurance. People cannot live in community without this element of trust. Rahner goes so far as to say that without this trust a person is not a Christian.[23] When we approach others with such trust, we are taking it for granted that they are not less worthy or less upright than we consider ourselves to be. It is only when we have an obvious self-critical understanding of ourselves that we can approach others without a sense of pride. When such self-critical behaviour has become part of who we are, we gain a sense of personal freedom in which we no longer see ourselves as the criterion of truth. This sense of freedom makes us ready to serve others fully. Rahner makes this point in the following statement:

> Only if we succeed in this do we become free from the most deeply hidden self-alienation: that which confuses the most subjective ego with the true ego which is attained only by conquering ourselves, ultimately by reaching God, not merely by a cheap ideologizing of our own subjectivity but by really exposing ourselves to another by serving. It is by being willing to do this that we give our trust in advance.[24]

Trust is essential for any community. In the case of the church, if it is to be a community, this means trust in ourselves as free persons, and trust in ourselves as ministers. In regard to those who minister, this element of trust has a particular nuance, and it is in the dynamic of trust that service, the real gift of self to others, emerges. If we trust those whom we serve in our ministry, we have to grant others a prior claim on our own life and action. We must open ourselves to the other without any guarantee of their trustworthiness. We serve not knowing what the outcome will be. If we do not fully open ourselves to the other in service, then we do not trust them, but rely on our own knowledge of the other and of ourselves. This is a form of bias that presumes that we know what others' needs are before listening to them and what they believe their needs to be. We institutionalize their needs rather than relating to them as persons in trust and love, and seeing their specific concerns. Only trusting, loving relationships can foster the type of community in which such service can flourish.

Not all people see the church functioning as this type of community. They are dissatisfied, not because of egotistical or selfish motives, but because they realize that the church does not meet their natural, deep need for belonging and being accepted. They see the church as an institutionally organized structure that does not fulfill the interconnectedness and interdependence of life that is expressed in the classical doctrines of revelation, christology, and trinity. The God that Christians confess their faith in is a communitarian God, a God who is constituted by the welcoming love of Father, Son, and Holy Spirit. Our God is a creator who does not want to be alone, but who wants to have covenant partners; our God is a liberator who has inaugurated a new freedom for a relationship with a God who is our Abba, and our God is a Holy Spirit who empowers a new community of freedom. This hunger for community is not a whim of the contemporary mindset; it is a longing of people to be fully who they are as God's created beings. It is a longing, as Migliore points out, to remind ourselves of who we are called to be as church.

> Any call for renewal in the church today does not derive from 'a craze for modernity' but from a fresh apprehension of the Gospel that gave the church its life....The mystery of the church is that it is called to share in the trinitarian love of God, the God who gives existence to others, shares life and power, and lives in the natural giving and receiving of love. The church is called to be the beginning of new human relationships, solidarity, and friendship beyond all privatism, classism, racism, sexism, and elitism.[25]

The church has to be evaluated by whether or not it helps people to become more fully human. Any system that denies people the fullest opportunity to attain their basic human freedom and dignity has no place in Christianity. Too many people have abandoned the church in search of a deeper meaning in life—they have gone in search of community. This was foreseen by the bishops at Vatican II, who realized that the renewal in the church and hope for its future mean returning to the gospel message and making it relevant to people's lives. Rooted in our humanity is a deep human need for personal contact. A resurgence in the church will not come about by more efficient organizational strategies, but only through the power of the Holy Spirit, in faith in the Risen Christ, and in building communities of the local church that live out Jesus' teaching of human freedom.

Jesus captivated people by his message of freedom and personal dignity for everyone. His disciples were his friends with whom he shared everything. They knew instinctively that what he was offering them was different from that of any of the institutions of their day. The God in Jesus spoke to the God in them, and this was the meeting of the dignity of both. His message was clear: he convinced them that they were special, not only in his eyes, but in God's as well. For centuries the church has fostered the opposite by telling people how sinful and unworthy they are in God's eyes. This is in direct contrast to Jesus' message, and to early church teaching. St. Irenaeus' (d. 200) most important contribution to theological anthropology was the idea that creation is not sinful by nature but, rather, distorted by sin. Although we are capable of sinning, we are not naturally sinful: we are created in the image of God. It is not surprising, then, that so many people in the church today do not feel the same joy and hope of the early community. The Second Vatican Council tried to get back to this Spirit-filled church by proclaiming that our hope, based on faith, is the source of our joy. It realized that our human dignity is intimately bound to our understanding of how we see ourselves as church community.

> What does the Church think of [humanity]? What recommendations seem needful for the upbuilding of contemporary society? What is the ultimate significance of human activity throughout the world? People are waiting for an answer to these questions. From the answers it will be increasingly clear that the People of God and the human race in whose midst it lives render service to each other. Thus the mission of the Church will show its religious, and by that very fact, its supremely human character. (GS 11)

The insight that our human dignity is intimately bound to our understanding of how we see ourselves as church community has a corollary: how we function as a church community reflects what we believe about the human person. This raises an obvious question: Is our church a living image of the communitarian God that we profess?

It is difficult to be convinced of this in the area of pastoral ministry. The church's current perspective on who can and who cannot minister, and why, is not fully reflective of a belief in the value of each person as created in the image of God. Yet the command to minister is embedded in our Christian understanding of the human person.

We are still waiting for answers to the questions posed by *Gaudium et Spes* that make it increasingly clear that all of the People of God are empowered to render service to each other. While we wait, however, an intentional focus on theological anthropology can strengthen those who are already involved in ministry and can challenge the church to widen its mandate for those who can minister in its name. No one member of the church has all the gifts needed to serve the community. The fullness of the communitarian God, the Body of Christ, is in the entirety of the People of God.

Notes

Preface

1. *Catholic New Times,* Vol. 25, No. 2 (January 28, 2001), 1.
2. *Lay Pastoral Associates in Parish Settings: Perspectives, Considerations and Suggestions* (Toronto: Ontario Conference of Catholic Bishops, 1999).
3. Ibid., 7.
4. *Guidelines for the Employment of Lay Pastoral Ministers* (Toronto:Archdiocese ofToronto, 1996).
5. "Dogmatic Constitution on the Church" (*Lumen Gentium*) in *The Documents of Vatican II.* Walter M.Abbot, General Editor (Chicago: Follett, 1966).
6. *Guidelines for the Employment of Lay Pastoral Ministers,* op. cit., ii.
7. Ibid., 5.

Introduction

1. HerbertVorgrimler, *Sacramental Theology* (Collegeville, MN: Liturgical Press, 1992), 237.

Chapter 1

1. "The Pastoral Constitution on the Church in the Modern World" (*Gaudium et Spes)* in *The Documents ofVatican II.* Walter M.Abbott, General Editor (Chicago:Follett, 1966), 17.
2. "The Declaration on Religious Freedom" (*Dignitatis Humanae)* in *The Documents ofVatican II,* Abbott, 1.
3. See Richard McBrien, *Catholicism.* Study Edition (San Francisco: Harper and Row, 1981), 64–65.
4. Mary M. Garascia, "Theological Anthropology," in *The College Student's Introduction to Theology* (Collegeville, MN: Liturgical Press, 1993), 123.
5. Catherine Mowry La Cugna, *God for Us:The Trinity and Christian Life* (San Francisco: Harper, 1991), 247.
6. St.Thomas Aquinas, *Summa Theologica.* Complete English edition in five volumes. Translated by the Fathers of the English Dominican province. Volume 1. (Westminster, MD: Christian Classics, 1981).
7. La Cugna, 250–251.
8. Ibid., 251.

9   Thomas Groome, *What Makes Us Catholic: Eight Gifts for Life* (San Francisco: Harper, 2002), 60.

10   Ibid., 58.

11   Garascia, 125.

12   See "The Dignity of Persons and the Catholic Intellectual Vision" by Brian F. Linnane, S.J., in *As Leaven in the World: Catholic Perspectives on Faith, Vocation, and the Intellectual Life,* Thomas M. Landy, ed. (Franklin, WI: Sheed and Ward, 2001), 200.

13   Karl Rahner, *Foundations of Christian Faith: An Introduction to the Idea of Christianity* (New York: Crossroad, 1985), 39.

14   Groome, op. cit., 66.

15   McBrien, *Catholicism*, 141.

16   Groome, 54.

17   "Church Order," by David Power, OMI, in *The New Dictionary of Sacramental Worship,* Peter E. Fink, S.J., ed. (Collegeville, MN: Liturgical Press, 1990), 230.

Chapter 2

1   "The Dogmatic Constitution on Divine Revelation" (*Dei Verbum*), Abbott, 107–132.

2   Neil Ormerod, *Introducing Contemporary Theologies: The What and Who of Theology Today.* Rev. ed. (New York: Orbis, 1997), 108–109.

3   Avery Dulles, "Faith and Revelation," in *Systematic Theology: Roman Catholic Perspectives,* Volume 1, Francis Schussler Fiorenza and John P. Galvin, eds. (Minneapolis, MN: Fortress, 1991), 116.

4   ———. *Revelation Theology: A History* (New York: Herder and Herder, 1972), 157.

5   For a fuller description of this discussion, see Chapter 5, "Christian Faith: A Contemporary View," by John R. Connolly in *The College Student's Introduction to Theology,* Thomas P. Rausch, ed. (Collegeville, MN: Liturgical Press, 1993), 91–106.

6   Rahner, *Foundations of Christian Faith,* 140–142.

7   Ibid., 24.

8   Ibid., 185.

9   Ormerod, 108–109.

10   Kathryn Tanner, *Jesus, Humanity and the Trinity* (Minneapolis, MN: Fortress Press, 2001), 42.

11   Rahner, *Foundations of Christian Faith,* 173.

12   Rene Latrourelle, *Theology of Revelation* (Staten Island, NY: Alba House, 1966), 485.

13   "The Dogmatic Constitution on Divine Revelation" (*Dei Verbum*), op. cit.

14   Rahner, *Foundations of Christian Faith,* 140.

15   Ibid., 39.

16   Ibid., 162.

17   Ibid., 152.

18   Bernard Lonergan, *Method in Theology* (Minneapolis, MN: Seabury Press, 1972), 109.

19   E.M. Good, "Love in the Old Testament," in *The Interpreter's Dictionary of the Bible,* Volume 3, George Arthur Buttrick, ed. (Nashville: Abingdon, 1980), 164.

20   Ibid., 167.

21   Karl Lehmann, ed., *Karl Rahner, The Content of Faith: The Best of Karl Rahner's Theological Writings* (New York: Crossroad, 1999), 252.

22   Ibid., 255.
23   Canadian Conference of Catholic Bishops, *Catechism of the Catholic Church* (Ottawa: Publications Service, 1992), #218.
24   Lehmann, 256.
25   Ibid., 256.
26   "By calling God 'Father,' the language of faith indicates two main things: God is the first origin of everything and transcendent authority; and that [God] is at the same time goodness and loving care for all [God's] children. God's parental tenderness can also be expressed in the image of motherhood (cf. Isa. 66:13; Ps 131:2-6) which emphasizes God's immanence, the intimacy between Creator and creature.... [God] is neither man nor woman: [God] is God." *Catechism* #239.
27   G. Johnston, "Love in the New Testament," in *The Interpreter's Dictionary of the Bible,* Volume 3, 169.
28   See N. W. Porteous, "Image of God," in *The Interpreter's Dictionary of the Bible,* Volume 2, 682-685.
29   *Catechism, #356.*
30   Richard P. McBrien, ed., *The Harper Collins Encyclopedia of Catholicism* (San Francisco: Harper, 1995), 654.
31   Karl Rahner and Herbert Vorgrimler, *Dictionary of Theology. Second Edition* (New York: Crossroad, 1985), 228.
32   Porteous, 685.
33   Ibid., 685.
34   Rahner and Vorgrimler, 228.
35   Daniel L. Migliore, *Faith Seeking Understanding: An Introduction to Christian Theology.* (Grand Rapids, MI: Eerdman's, 1991), 121.
36   Ibid., 121.
37   Ibid., 122.
38   McBrien, *The Harper Collins Encyclopedia of Catholicism,* 654.
39   Migliore, 122-123.
40   Sallie McFague, *Models of God: Theology for an Ecological, Nuclear Age* (Philadelphia: Fortress, 1987), 136.
41   Migliore, 124.
42   Ibid., 125.
43   See Rosemary Radford Ruether, *Sexism and God-Talk: Toward a Feminist Theology* (Boston: Beacon Press, 1983), 103.
44   McFague, 130.
45   Ibid., 130.
46   Ibid., 128.
47   Ibid., 129.
48   Migliore, 131.
49   Ibid., 132.
50   Ibid., 132.
51   Richard J. Hauser, S.J., "Each Mortal Thing Does One Thing and the Same— Selves: An Approach to Christian Discernment," in *Handbook of Spirituality for Ministers,* Robert J. Wicks, ed. (New York: Paulist Press, 1995), 223.

52 McBrien, *Catholicism*, 977.
53 Jude Winkler, O.F.M. Conv. "Ministry in the New Testament," in *Handbook of Spirituality for Ministers,* 339.
54 Ibid., 331.

Chapter 3

1   Rahner, *Foundations of Christian Faith,* 225-226.
2   McBrien, *The Harper Collins Encyclopedia of Catholicism,* 311.
3   It was precisely such a denial of the fullness of Jesus' humanity that gave rise to the early Christian heresies of Docetism and Gnosticism. Docetism held that Jesus only "seemed" to have a human body, and Gnosticism denied the goodness of the created and material world. Later on, Arianism, named after Arius, the Alexandrian priest, was declared heretical by the church council at Nicea in 325 for denying the true divinity of Christ. In response to the Arian controversy, the council affirmed the divinity of Jesus. In 451, the council of Chalcedon, responding to other christological controversies that arose after Nicea, affirmed the dual nature of Jesus: that is, that he was truly man and truly God. In Jesus, there are two natures, human and divine, united in one person.
4   Rahner, *Foundations of Christian Faith,* 177.
5   Dermot Lane, *The Reality of Jesus* (New York: Paulist Press, 1975), 10.
6   Rahner, *Foundations of Christian Faith,* 307.
7   Tanner, 57.
8   Ibid., 224.
9   Ibid., 225.
10 Lehmann, *Karl Rahner, Content of Faith,* 348.
11 Albert Nolan, *Jesus Before Christianity* (New York: Orbis, 1976), 166.
12 See Lane, 32-43.
13 Monika Hellwig, *Jesus: The Compassion of God.* (Wilmington, DE: Michael Glazier, 1983), 90.
14 Ibid., 88.
15 Ibid., 95-96.
16 Ibid., 99.
17 *Catechism,* #1723.
18 See Richard Rohr with John Bookser Feister, *Jesus' Plan for a New World Order: The Sermon on the Mount* (Cincinnati, OH: St. Anthony Messenger Press, 1996). I rely on Chapter 8 for my exposition of the challenge of the Beatitudes.
19 Rohr points out that most bibles soften this Beatitude by using the words "right" or "righteousness" instead of "justice," but the word in Greek clearly means "justice." Rohr, 134.
20 Ibid., 137.
21 Ibid., 140.
22 Ibid., 142.
23 Ibid., 143.
24 William Thompson, *The Jesus Debate: A Survey and Synthesis* (New York: Paulist, 1985), 203-205.

25 Ibid., 203.
26 See C.W.F. Smith, "Lord's Prayer," in *The Interpreter's Dictionary of the Bible,* Volume 3, 154-158.
27 "Forgiveness meant the cancellation or remission of one's debts to God. To forgive in Greek *(aphiemi)* means to remit, release or liberate." Nolan, 48.
28 An understanding of the root of the word "believe" is helpful here. In both Greek and Latin its roots mean "to give one's heart to." The heart is the self at its deepest level. To have faith in someone means involvement at a much deeper level than intellectual assent. To have faith in God and Jesus means giving one's heart—one's self at its deepest level—to him as our Lord and our God. See: Marcus J. Borg, *Meeting Jesus Again for the First Time* (San Francisco: Harper, 1994), 137.
29 Nolan, 51.
30 McBrien, *The Harper Collins Encyclopedia of Catholicism,* 74.
31 M.H. Shepherd, Jr., "Apostle," in *The Interpreter's Dictionary of the Bible,* Volume 1, 170-172.
32 Ibid., 172.
33 Rahner, *Foundations of Christian Faith,* 310.
34 Borg, 135.
35 Kenan Osborne, OFM. *Ministry: Lay Ministry in the Roman Catholic Church* (New York: Paulist, 1993), 49.
36 Ibid., 49.

Chapter 4

1   Lehmann, *Karl Rahner, The Content of Faith,* 357.
2   See William Placher, "The Triune God: The *Perichoresis* of Particular Persons," in *Theology After Liberalism: A Reader,* John W. Webster and George P. Schner, eds. (Oxford: Blackwell, 2000).
3   Alister McGrath, *Christian Theology: An Introduction* (Oxford: Blackwell, 1994), 255.
4   McBrien, *Catholicism,* 346.
5   See McGrath, 248-249.
6   Ibid., 208-213.
7   Ibid., 250.
8   Leonardo Boff, *Holy Trinity, Perfect Community* (Maryknoll, NY: Orbis, 2000), 50.
9   Ibid., 15.
10 Both sides of this debate were not entirely unanimous, however. Cyril of Alexandria spoke of the Spirit as belonging to the Son, and the early Christian writers were deliberately vague about the precise role of the Spirit within the Godhead (see McGrath, 266-269). Also, St. Augustine begins his explanation of the Trinity not with the three persons, but with the one nature or substance. He insists that the Father and the Son in the procession of the Spirit act as one principle. This is aligned with the Greek tendency to consider the Father as the one supreme principle. (See Chapter IV, "Relations of Origin: The 'Processions' in God" in Bertrand de Margerie, *The Christian Trinity in History,* Still River, MA: St. Bede's Publications, 1975.)
11 Lehmann, *Karl Rahner, The Content of Faith,* 362.

[12] Ibid., 356.

[13] La Cugna, 296-297.

[14] Ibid., 292.

[15] Thus, the original use of the term referred to all forms of ministry or service, official or unofficial, that a person provided on behalf of the church in general, or to an individual. The recent use of the term to refer to those especially ordained for a specific service is a limited use of its original intent.

[16] Jurgen Moltmann, *The Trinity and the Kingdom: The Doctrine of God,* Margaret Kohl, trans. (San Francisco: Harper, 1981), 198.

Chapter 5

[1] Groome, 85.

[2] Edward J. Kilmartin, "Theology of the Sacraments: Toward a New Understanding of the Chief Rites of the Church of Jesus Christ," in *Alternative Futures for Worship, Vol 1.* Edited by Regis Duffy (Collegeville, MN: Liturgical Press, 1987), 141-142.

[3] This is an observation that is often missed when we talk about religious expression. In many cases, the opposite is advocated: the goal is somehow to transcend our bodiliness and express ourselves in some spiritual realm that is disjointed from our bodies. Understanding the human spirit as expressed in bodiliness suggests that our self-transcendence is within our human, bodily existence.

[4] For some of the ways in which the sacraments relate to the daily reality of our lives, see Leonardo Boff, *Sacraments of Life, Life of the Sacraments* (Beltsville, MD: Pastoral Press, 1987).

[5] Kilmartin, 142.

[6] Ibid., 143.

[7] Karl Rahner, "The Theology of Symbol," in *Theological Investigations,* Vol. IV (Baltimore: Helicon, 1966), 224.

[8] If the symbolic nature of the sacraments is not realized, then we have empty symbols that render little or no meaning, or empty rituals that have become routine rather than celebratory.

[9] Karl Rahner, ed., *Encyclopedia of Theology: The Concise Sacramentum Mundi* (New York: Seabury, 1975), 1485.

[10] See McBrien, *The Harper Collins Encyclopedia of Catholicism,* 1146.

[11] Ibid., 1147.

[12] Liturgy refers to the whole range of actions, words of praise, and thanksgiving that the faith community gives to God. Sacraments, on the other hand, are highly focused action-words within the liturgical context. Many contemporary authors believe that "liturgy" is a more encompassing term than "sacrament" to denote God's grace permeating our reality.

[13] Groome, 84-85.

[14] In identifying Jesus as the primordial sacrament, it is helpful to make the following distinctions for the term "sacrament":
Sacrament: Jesus Christ, sign of salvation, who works salvation.

sacrament: The church, sign of salvation, which works salvation as instrument of Jesus Christ. A sacrament is worldly reality that reveals the mystery of salvation, because it is its realization.

sacraments: The seven sacred signs instituted by Jesus, and determined by the church, to be used by the church for our salvation.

sacramentals: A sign, similar to a sacrament, determined by the church as a means to help us toward our salvation. They do not carry the guarantee of grace associated with the seven sacraments. Examples are holy water, crucifixes, and palm branches used on Palm Sunday.

[15] Ray R. Noll, *Sacraments: A New Understanding for a New Generation* (Mystic, CT: Twenty-Third Publications, 1999), 20.

[16] Vorgrimler tells us that Carl Feckes (d. 1958) was the first person in the twentieth century who, in renewing these ideas, called Jesus Christ the "primordial sacrament" on whom rests the sacramental world of the church and the individual sacraments. In the spirit of renewed Thomism, and under the influence of an existential philosophy of encounter (experience of the other), Edward Schillebeeckx (b. 1914) described Jesus Christ as the sacrament of the encounter with God. The interpretation of Jesus as primordial sacrament is generally accepted (Vorgrimler, *Sacramental Theology*, 32).

[17] Ibid., 31.

[18] Ibid., 31.

[19] Edward Schillebeeckx, *Christ the Sacrament of the Encounter with God* (Kansas City: Sheed, Andrews and McMeel, 1963), 15.

[20] The Dogmatic Constitution on the Church (*Lumen Gentium*), Abbott, 15.

[21] Vorgrimler, *Sacramental Theology*, 37.

[22] Karl Rahner, *The Church and the Sacraments* (Edinburgh/London: Herder, 1963), 18.

[23] Vorgrimler, *Sacramental Theology*, 103.

[24] See *Baptism, Eucharist and Ministry* (Geneva: World Council of Churches, 1982), 2.

[25] Ibid., 2.

[26] Groome, 86.

[27] See Philippe Beguerie and Claude Duchsneau, *How to Understand the Sacraments* (London: SCM Press, 1993), 85.

[28] Ibid., 85.

[29] The Body and Blood of Jesus and his sacrificial death become present in the community's sacrifice through the consecration pronounced by the presider. Jesus' own words of institution spoken by the presider are the 'form.' The bread and wine are the 'matter,' and this consecration is understood as a genuine change of one substance (that of wheaten bread and grape wine) into another (namely the flesh and blood of Jesus). This is what we mean by *transubstantiation.* (Rahner/Vorgrimler, *Dictionary of Theology*, 156).

[30] *Baptism, Eucharist and Ministry*, 14.

[31] Ibid., 14.

[32] Migliore, 224–225.

[33] See Jeffrey Vanderwilt, *A Church Without Borders: The Eucharist and the Church in Ecumenical Perspective* (Collegeville, MN: Liturgical Press, 1998).

Chapter 6

1. "These four characteristics, inseparably linked with each other, indicate essential features of the church and her mission. The church does not possess them of herself; it is Christ, who, through the Holy Spirit makes his church one, holy, catholic and apostolic; and it is he who calls her to realize each of these qualities." (*Catechism of the Catholic Church*, #811)

2. McBrien, *Catholicism*, 714.

3. "Church," by Michael Fahey in *Systematic Theology: Roman Catholic Perspectives*, Vol. II, 19.

4. McBrien, *Catholicism*, 578.

5. See "Church," by P.S. Minear, in *The Interpreter's Dictionary of the Bible*, Vol. 1, 607-617.

6. Raymond Brown's study of these early communities concludes that none of them had broken *koinonia*, or communion, with one another. See Raymond Brown, *The Churches the Apostles Left Behind* (New York: Paulist, 1984).

7. Miroslav Volf, *After Our Likeness: The Church as Image of the Trinity* (Grand Rapids, MI: Eerdmans), 1998.

8. Minear, 611.

9. It cannot be overstressed that the Christian community as the new "People of God" does not annul the first covenant of God given to Israel. Israel will always be God's people, and the Jews remain the people whom God first addressed (see Fahey, 37).

10. For further elaboration of the image of the Body of Christ, see Minear, 615.

11. La Cugna, 402.

12. McBrien, *Catholicism*, 592.

13. "Constitution on the Sacred Liturgy" (*Sacrosanctum Concilium*), Abbott, 133-182.

14. See "Ministry," by Joseph M. Powers, S.J., in *The New Dictionary of Sacramental Worship*, 828-837.

15. "Decree on the Apostolate of the Laity" (*Apostolicam Actuositatem*), Abbott, 486-525.

16. "Laity," by Martin H. Work, in Abbott, 486.

17. Volf, 231.

18. Ibid., 226-246.

19. See Karl Rahner, *The Practice of Faith: A Handbook of Contemporary Spirituality* (New York: Crossroad, 1986), especially "New Offices and Ministries in the Church," 191-193.

20. Ibid., 192.

21. Fahey, 10-11.

22. The great Christian mystic and author Thomas Merton addressed this issue at the Bangkok conference on December 10, 1968. Thomas Merton, *The Bangkok Conference* (Kansas City, MO: Credence Cassettes), *National Catholic Reporter*, undated.

23. Lehmann, 480-81.

24. Ibid., 482-83.

25. Migliore, 188-89.

Bibliography

Abbott, Walter M., ed. *The Documents of Vatican II*. Chicago: Follett, 1966.

Aquinas, Thomas. *Summa Theologica*. Complete English edition in five volumes. Translated by the Fathers of the English Dominican Province. Volume 1. Westminster, MD: Christian Classics, 1981.

Beguerie, Philippe and Claude Duchesneau. *How to Understand the Sacraments*. London: SCM Press, 1993.

Boff, Leonardo. *Holy Trinity, Perfect Community*. Maryknoll, NY: Orbis, 2000.

————. *Sacraments of Life, Life of the Sacraments*. Beltsville, MD: Pastoral Press, 1987.

Bokenkotter, Thomas. *Essential Catholicism: Dynamics of Faith and Belief*. New York: Doubleday, 1985.

Borg, Marcus J. *Meeting Jesus Again for the First Time*. San Francisco: Harper, 1995.

Brown, Raymond. *The Churches the Apostles Left Behind*. New York: Paulist, 1984.

Buckley, Michael. "Back to the Basics with faith, hope, and love." *The Universe* 9/01.

Clifford, Anne M. *Introducing Feminist Theology*. Maryknoll, NY: Orbis, 2001.

Cooke, Bernard. *Sacraments and Sacramentality*. Mystic, CT: Twenty-Third Publications, 1995.

de Margerie, Bertrand. *The Christian Trinity in History*. Still River, MA: St. Bede's Publications, 1975.

Donovan, Daniel. *What Are They Saying About Ministerial Priesthood?* New York: Paulist Press, 1992.

Doyle, Dennis H. "The Trinity and Catholic Intellectual Life." In *As Leaven in the World: Catholic Perspectives on Faith, Vocation, and the Intellectual Life*. Edited by Thomas M. Landy. Franklin, WI: Sheed and Ward, 2001.

Dulles, Avery. "Faith and Revelation." In *Systematic Theology: Roman Catholic Perspectives,* Volume 1, edited by Francis Schussler Fiorenza and John P. Galvin. Minneapolis: Fortress Press, 1991.

————. *Revelation and Theology: A History.* New York: Herder and Herder, 1972.

Fahey, Michael. "Church." In *Systematic Theology: Roman Catholic Perspectives,* Volume II, edited by Francis Schussler Fiorenza and John P. Galvin. Minneapolis: Fortress, 1991.

Garascia, Mary M. "Theological Anthropology." In *The College Student's Introduction to Theology,* edited by Thomas P. Rausch. Collegeville, MN: Fortress Press, 1991.

Groome, Thomas. *What Makes Us Catholic: Eight Gifts for Life.* San Francisco: Harper, 2002.

Helwig, Monika. *Jesus: The Compassion of God.* Wilmington, DE: Michael Glazier, 1985.

————. *The Eucharist and the Hunger of the World.* New York: Paulist Press, 1976.

Hill, Brennan R., Paul Knitter and William Madges. *Faith, Religion, and Theology: A Contemporary Introduction.* Rev. ed. Mystic, CT: Twenty-Third Publications, 1997.

Kilmartin, Edward J. "Theology of the Sacraments: Toward a New Understanding of the Chief Rites of the Church of Jesus Christ." In *Alternative Futures for Worship,* Volume 1, edited by Regis A. Duffy. Collegeville, MN: Liturgical Press, 1987.

Kolvenbach, Peter-Hans. "Laity and Women in the Church of the Millenium." *Review of Ignatian Spirituality: Bulletin of the Council on Ignatian Spirituality* xxx, ii/1999/ 91:21-30.

Kung, Hans. *The Church.* New York: Image Books, 1976.

La Cugna, Catherine Mowry. *God for Us: The Trinity and the Christian Life.* San Francisco: Harper, 1991.

Lane, Dermot A. *The Reality of Jesus.* New York: Paulist Press, 1975.

Latourelle, Rene. *Theology of Revelation.* Staten Island, NY: Alba House, 1966.

Lehmann, Karl, Albert Raffelt and Harvey D. Egan, eds. *Karl Rahner, The Content of Faith: The Best of Karl Rahner's Theological Writings.* New York: Crossroad, 1999.

Linnane, Brian F. "The Dignity of Persons and the Catholic Intellectual Vision." in *As Leaven in the World: Catholic Perspectives on Faith, Vocation, and the Intellectual Life,* edited by Thomas M. Landy. Franklin, WI: Sheed and Ward, 2001.

Lonergan, Bernard. *Method in Theology.* Minneapolis, MN: Seabury Press, 1972.

Martos, Jos. *Doors to the Sacred: An Historical Introduction to the Sacraments in the Catholic Church.* Rev. ed. Ligouri, MO: Triumph Books, 2001.

McBrien, Richard P. *Catholicism.* Study Ed. San Francisco: Harper and Row, 1981.

McFague, Sallie. *Models of God: Theology for an Ecological, Nuclear Age.* Philadelphia: Fortress Press, 1987.

McGrath, Alister. *Christian Theology: An Introduction.* Oxford: Blackwell, 1994.

Menoud, P.H. "Church Life and Organization." In *The Interpreter's Dictionary of the Bible,* Volume 1. Nashville: Abingdon, 1962.

Merton, Thomas. *The Bangkok Conference.* Kansas City, MO: Credence Cassettes, *National Catholic Reporter,* undated.

Migliore, Daniel L. *Faith Seeking Understanding: An Introduction to Christian Theology.* Grand Rapids, MI: Eerdmans, 1991.

Minear, P.S. "Church, the idea of." In *The Interpreter's Dictionary of the Bible,* Volume 1, edited by George Arthur Buttrick. Nashville: Abingdon, 1962.

Moltmann, Jurgen. *The Trinity and the Kingdom: The Doctrine of God.* Translated by Margaret Kohl. San Francisco: Harper and Row, 1981.

Nolan, Albert. *Jesus Before Christianity.* Rev. ed. Maryknoll, NY: Orbis, 1992.

Noll, Ray R. *Sacraments: A New Understanding for a New Generation.* Mystic, CT: Twenty-Third Publications, 1999.

O'Collins, Gerald. *What Are They Saying About Jesus?* 2nd ed. New York: Paulist Press 1977.

Ormerod, Neil. *Introducing Contemporary Theologies: The What and the Who of Theology Today.* Maryknoll, NY: Orbis, 1997.

Osborne, Kenan. *Lay Ministry in the Roman Catholic Church: Its History and Theology.* New York: Paulist, 1993.

———. *Sacramental Theology: A General Introduction.* New York: Paulist Press, 1998.

Pelikan, Jaroslav. *The Christian Tradition: A History of the Development of Doctrine,* Volume I. Chicago: University of Chicago Press, 1989.

Placher, William. "The Triune God: The *Perichoresis* of Particular Persons." In *Theology After Liberalism,* edited by John Webster and George P. Schner. Oxford: Blackwell, 2000.

Power, David N. "Church Order." In *The New Dictionary of Sacramental Worship,* edited by Peter E. Fink. Collegeville, MN: Liturgical Press, 1990.

——— et al. "Current Theology. Sacramental Theology: A Review of Literature." *Theological Studies* 55 (1994):657-705.

Powers, Joseph M. "Ministry." In *The New Dictionary of Sacramental Worship,* edited by Peter E. Fink. Collegeville, MN: Liturgical Press, 1990.

Rahner, Karl. *Foundations of Christian Faith: An Introduction to the Idea of Christianity.* New York: Crossroad, 1985.

———. *The Christian of the Future.* Freiburg: Herder, 1967.

———. *The Church and the Sacraments.* Edinburgh-London: Herder, 1963.

———. *The Practice of Faith: A Handbook of Contemporary Spirituality.* New York: Crossroad, 1986.

————. "The Theology of Symbol." In *Theological Investigations,* Volume IV. Baltimore: Helicon, 1966.

————, ed. *Encyclopedia of Theology: The Concise Sacramentum Mundi.* New York: Seabury, 1975.

Rohr, Richard with John Bookser Feister. *Jesus' Plan for a New World: The Sermon on the Mount.* Cincinnati, OH: St. Anthony Messenger Press, 1996.

Ruether, Rosemary Radford. *To Change the World: Christology and Cultural Criticism.* London: SCM Press, 1981.

Schillebeeckx, Edward. *Christ the Sacrament of the Encounter with God.* Kansas City: Sheed, Andrews and McMeel, 1963.

Shepherd, Jr., M.H. "Apostle." In *The Interpreter's Dictionary of the Bible,* Volume I, edited by George Arthur Buttrick. Nashville: Abingdon, 1962.

————. "Ministry, Christian." In *The Interpreter's Dictionary of the Bible,* Volume 3, edited by George Athur Buttrick. Nashville: Abingdon, 1962.

Smith, C.W.F. "Lord's Prayer." In *The Interpreter's Dictionary of the Bible,* Volume 3, edited by George Arthur Buttrick. Nashville: Abingdon: 1962.

Tanner, Kathryn. *Jesus, Humanity, and the Trinity: A Brief Systematic Theology.* Minneapolis: Fortress Press, 2001.

Tavard, George H. *A Theology for Ministry* in *Theology and Life Series, 6.* Wilmington, DE: Michael Glazier, 1983.

————. *The Church, Community of Salvation: An Ecumenical Ecclesiology.* Collegeville, MN: Liturgical Press, 1992.

————. *The Church Tomorrow.* New York: Herder and Herder, 1965.

————. *The Pilgrim Church.* New York: Herder and Herder, 1967.

————. "Ordination of Women," in *The New Dictionary of Sacramental Worship,* edited by Peter E. Fink. Collegeville, MN: Liturgical Press, 1990, 910-915.

————. *Woman in Christian Tradition.* Notre Dame, IN: University of Notre Dame Press, 1973.

Thompson, William M. *The Jesus Debate.* New York: Paulist, 1985.

Vanderwilt, Jeffrey. *A Church Without Borders: The Eucharist and the Church in Ecumenical Perspective.* Collegeville, MN: Liturgical Press, 1998

Volf, Miroslav. *After Our Likeness: The Church as the Image of the Trinity.* Grand Rapids, MI: Eerdmans, 1998.

Vorgrimler, Herbert. *Sacramental Theology.* Collegeville, MN: Liturgical Press, 1992.

Wicks, Robert, editor. *Handbook of Spirituality for Ministers.* New York: Paulist, 1995.

World Council of Churches. *Baptism, Eucharist and Ministry.* Geneva, 1982.

Glossary

Anthropology
From the Greek *anthropos* meaning 'human being.' The study of the origins and development of human existence.

Anthropology, Theological
The study of the origins and development of the human person in the context of Christian belief.

Apostle
From the Greek *apostolis* meaning 'one who is sent,' a messenger. An office of the church in the New Testament period.

Baptism
From the Greek *baptizein* meaning to immerse. The sacrament of initiation into the Christian community. It is the first and fundamental sacrament.

Basileia
A Greek translation of the Aramaic word meaning 'God's rule,' or 'reign of God.' The *basileia* of God is the substance of Jesus' message.

Charism
A spiritual gift given to a person by the Holy Spirit for the good of the community.

Christology
The theological study of Jesus Christ. It is the branch of systematic theology which asks such questions as: Who is Jesus? Why is he believed to be the messiah?

Conversion
Meaning literally ' to turn away from.' The fundamental change when a person turns away from sinful ways toward deeper intimacy with God, and a greater recognition of the presence and purpose of God in their life.

Covenant
A mutual bond, or agreement, between God and the people. It is initiated by God and freely entered into by the people.

Diakonia
From the Greek meaning 'service.' It refers to all types of ministry that people perform for the church community. Its recent use to refer to those especially ordained for a specific service is a limited use of its original intent.

Disciple
A follower of Jesus; meaning literally 'one who learns from.'

Doctrine
An official teaching of the church. Doctrine involves questioning, reflection, and the systematization of ideas.

Ecclesiology
The theological study of the church.

Ekklesia
The word 'church' is based on the Greek word *ekklesia*. An *ekklesia* was a legislative assembly of people to which only free citizens with full rights could belong. The original Greek term had no religious significance. It referred to the dignity of the people gathered, and to the legality of the assembly itself. Applied to the Christian community, *ekklesia* refers to a people who have been transformed to a new way of being human in relationship to God, and with others.

Enlightenment, The
The philosophical and scientific movement of the seventeenth and eighteenth centuries. Philosophical and religious writers of this period rejected tradition and authority in favour of human reason.

Eucharist
From the Greek *eucharistein,* meaning 'to give thanks.' It is the sacramental celebration of the Last Supper, and of the Paschal Mystery.

Faith
Personal acknowledgment of belief in God. It is the correlative of revelation. Revelation becomes actual only when it is accepted in faith by each believer.

Filioque
From the Latin meaning 'and from the Son.' The doctrine which states that the Holy Spirit proceeds from the Father and from the Son in a single principle.

Hermeneutics
The science of interpretation. When we seek to understand and interpret the meanings and values of our religious experience we engage in the theological task of hermeneutics, which is the interpretation of the Word of God in the Christian tradition.

Homoiousios
A Greek word meaning 'of a *similar* substance.' A trinitarian heresy according to which the Son's nature was not equal to but similar to that of the Father.

Homoousios
A Greek word meaning 'of the *same* substance.' The trinitarian doctrine that the Son and the Holy Spirit have the very same nature as the Father. It means that the Son is of equal status as the Father, and thus Jesus is truly God. This teaching was used at the Council of Nicea (325) to define the proper understanding of the divinity of Christ.

Hypostasis
A Greek word used to designate a Divine Person. It was used at times in trinitarian discussions of the third and fourth centuries in distinction from *ousia*, meaning 'being,' to help to clarify the three *hypostaseis* of God in one being.

Hypostatic Union
The union of the divine nature and the human nature of Jesus Christ in one Person, or hypostasis.

Imago Dei
A Latin term meaning 'image of God.' It is the theological concept that expresses the likeness of the human person to God. The whole person, body and soul, male and female, is created in God's image to be God's partner. (Gen 1:26-27)

Incarnation
From the Latin *in-carno*, literally 'in the flesh.' It is the self-revelation of the Word of God, the *Logos*, or Divine Word, in the world. The assuming of a human nature by God whereby God is made visible to us in the Incarnation of Jesus Christ.

Koinonia
A Greek word meaning 'togetherness' or 'loving union.' It is the communion produced by the Holy Spirit, and is a quality that should be characteristic of the community of the church as it was characteristic of the early church.

Logos
From the Greek meaning "word," "speech." The Logos is the pre-existing Word of God who formed all of Creation and who became flesh in the Incarnation of Jesus Christ.

Ministry
A public service grounded in the Gospel and performed on behalf of the Christian community for the promotion of the reign of God.

Monotheism
The affirmation and belief that there is only one God.

Mystery
From the Greek meaning 'secret.' A sacred mystery is something about which we would know nothing were it not for God revealing it to us, and which is not wholly intelligible even after such revelation. It is not something we cannot know, but something we cannot wholly know, since it 'goes beyond' our human understanding.

Perichoresis
Latin: *circumincession;* English: reciprocal interpenetration. It refers to the way in which the Persons of the Trinity are in relation to one another. Each Person dwells in the other. For example, the Son and the Holy Spirit are present in the Father, and the Father and the Son are present in the Holy Spirit.

Pneumatological
Relating to the Holy Spirit. *Pneumatology* is a Greek word meaning 'the study of the Spirit.' It relates to the branch of systematic theology which deals with the Person and work of the Holy Spirit.

Revelation
The self-disclosure and self-communication of God to humanity through creation and events, and especially in the person of Jesus Christ.

Sacrament, Fundamental
The church is the fundamental sacrament in the sense of making Jesus Christ present to the world. It will continue to be effective as long as it manifests this redemptive work of Jesus.

Sacrament, Primordial
Jesus is the first, or primordial sacrament, since he mediates God's presence in the world.

Sacraments
Specifically, the seven sacred signs instituted by Jesus Christ and determined by the church to be used by the church for our salvation.

Salvation
Salvation is the goal of creation. To be saved is to be fully united with God, and with one another in God.

Sin
The refusal to enter into full relationship with God, with others, and with creation. It is the deliberate individual, or social, infidelity to the will of God.

Soteriology
The theological study of the passion, death, and resurrection of Jesus Christ insofar as they bring about our salvation.

Systematic theology
The attempt to understand the realities of faith articulated in the doctrinal tradition of the church community.

Trinity, Economic
The reality of the three Divine Persons as they are for us in God's revelation in the world and in its history as acting for us so that we might share in trinitarian life.

Trinity, Immanent
The Trinity considered in itself; the reality of the three Divine Persons as they exist in mutual relationship.

Twelve, The
The disciples chosen by Jesus. All of the Twelve were apostles, but not all of the apostles were among the original Twelve.

Vatican II
An ecumenical council of the church held at the Vatican from 1962-1965 in which the pope and bishops met to discuss, rework, and reformulate church teaching. The decrees of the Council have had a great effect on modern theology and church practice.